Speak German in 90 Days: A Self Study Guide to Becoming Fluent
Copyright © Kevin Marx 2013

Also by Kevin Marx:

Speak Japanese in 90 Days: A Self Study Guide to Becoming Fluent (Volume 1)

Speak Japanese in 90 Days: A Self Study Guide to Becoming Fluent (Volume 2)

Japanese Study Guide: A Visual Reference for Beginning Japanese Grammar

Speak German NOW: The Go-To Guide for Essential German Basics

Conner and the Telescope: Children's Multilingual Picture Book

Table of Contents

Prepositions

Sentence Structure and Clauses

Adjectives

Intermediate Grammar

Numbers, Dates, and Time

How to Study

This book consists of 90 lessons that can be studied in one day each. Each lesson will present you with ten vocabulary words to memorize and most will also contain a grammar structure to memorize. To memorize vocabulary, please create note cards using the grammar and vocabulary from each daily lesson. It is important that you have access to your vocabulary at all times during the day.

On both sides of the card write the numbers 1-10. On one side write the English word and on the other side write the German equivalent. Read word number one **<u>out loud</u>**. Flip the card. Read the German equivalent word **<u>out loud.</u>** Go on to the second word. Do this at least ten times for each word. You may notice, by the tenth time, that you can remember some of the words without making any effort. Please note that **<u>out loud</u>** is bold and underlined. It is extremely important that you say the words **<u>out loud</u>**.

Do this **<u>at least</u>** three times a day. The more often you do it, the easier it will be to recall the words. At the end of the day, try to make a sentence with the words you've memorized, or simply use the sample sentences provided in this book. Making sentences with your vocabulary words is just as important as saying everything **<u>out loud.</u>** If you do these two simple things, your progress will be much faster.

Practice each new card along with the old ones every day until you are able to freely use the vocabulary words on your own. Review all vocabulary words at least once a week, even if you feel you have memorized them.

Your brain will play tricks on you, and you may begin to memorize the order of the words on the card, so it is important to mix the order up. Do the odd words, then do the even words. Do the words backwards. You can also switch the language you start with. Start on the English side to improve your speaking, start on the German side to improve your reading and listening. Say everything **<u>out loud</u>**.

Motivation

The most difficult thing about learning a language is actually taking the time to study. Languages are different than most subjects, in that you cannot cram the information in one sitting. You must study as *often* as possible rather than as *long* as possible. It is imperative that you study and practice **every day**. You will gain more benefit from studying every day for fifteen minutes than you will from studying two hours once a week.

Your motivation for learning German is very important. Ask yourself, why do I want to study German? Remind yourself of the reason. Tell yourself *I want to study German*. Say it, out loud, right now: *I want to study German!* It is all a matter of will. You may find yourself one day feeling lazy, your thoughts telling you to relax, to procrastinate. Do not let this happen to you. Do not give in to negativity. If you feel this is happening, remind yourself of why you want to speak German, remind yourself that you want to do this. You want to study. You want to improve.

It is my hope that you are able to finish this book in 90 days, however, everyone has different learning curves and busy lives, so if you find that it may take you 180, or even 360 days to finish this book, do not feel down. This book was designed to be done at your own pace. You can do it! Good luck!

Practicing

You perfect what you practice. If you play video games all day, you will get good at playing video games, if you read books all day, you will become a fast reader. The same goes for language, if you practice reading, you will increase your reading skill, if you practice listening, you will increase your listening skill, if you practice speaking, you will increase your speaking skill. The problem for most people learning a language is that they waste time doing written grammar exercises, which makes you good at passing tests, but doesn't improve your speaking.

In order to practice, you need someone to speak with. If you don't have a Japanese speaking friend to practice with, this can be difficult. The solution to this problem: talk to yourself. Look around you. What do you see? Do you see a window, a door, a person, a bird? If you know the name of it in Japanese, say it, **<u>out loud</u>**. Ask yourself, *What am I doing*? Think of as many things as possible: *I am sitting, I am breathing, I am reading, I am thinking*. Say it **<u>out loud</u>**. Ask yourself, *What did I do yesterday*? *What will I do tomorrow*? You must do this if you want to improve your speaking, **you must speak**.

Pronunciation

I urge you to find some native German speaking music or videos to watch, so you can experience native pronunciation. To practice your pronunciation, the **absolute** best method is listening to music and singing along, while reading the lyrics so you know what you are pronouncing. Have you ever noticed that accents seem to disappear when singing? By training with singing, your English accent will slowly disappear and you will sound more and more like a native German speaker. However, pronunciation is something that will take you years of practice. In all honesty, you will most likely never sound like a native speaker, no matter how long you study. The goal of practicing pronunciation is to be understood, you want your pronunciation to be good enough so that no one misunderstands what you are saying. But don't worry, having an accent is cool!

One thing you must get used to when speaking German is using your throat. In linguistics, these are called Glottal sounds, and they are really a lot of fun! An example of this is the *ch* sound in German. This sound is the same one you make when you are trying to clear the back of your throat. It's like making the sound of a K, but continue breathing air out. It's important not to confuse this sound with *sh* in English, like many English speakers do. The *sh* in English is made with the front of your mouth, the *ch* in German is made with the back of your throat. Try practicing right now!

Most letters in German have a similar pronunciation to English, but some are different, and there are a few new letters to learn. The two dots above the ä, ö, ü, are called an *umlauts*. If you have trouble typing the umlaut on a computer, you can also write ae, oe, ue. Ä can sound soft like *eh* in *enter*, or hard like *ay* in *play*. The Ö and Ü sounds are somewhat more difficult, because these sounds don't exist in English. These sounds require you to round your lips like you are whistling. Ö sounds a bit like the *oo* in *cool*. Another trick to make this sound is to round your lips like you are whistling and say the letter A. Ü sounds a bit like the *ou* in *you*. Another trick to make this sound is to round your lips like you are whistling and say the letter E.

Some consonants change their pronunciation depending on their position in a word, at the beginning or the end. At the beginning of a word they are voiced, at the end they are not voiced. An example is D(voiced) and T(not voiced). In the name *Dieter*, the D is voiced, but in the word *Mond*(mouth), the D sounds like a T. D and T use the same mouth, tongue, throat, and lip movements, the only difference between making these sounds is using your voice or not. Here are a few more examples of voiced and unvoiced sounds in English.

Voiced→Unvoiced
B→P
D→T
G→K
Z→S

The following list will give you the basics of pronunciation. Again, this list is just for your reference, you really need to listen to these words being spoken. So get out there, go on the internet and find some music, or a video, or find a German friend! What are you doing? Go now!

German Letter	English Pronunciation	Example German Word	English Pronunciation
a	ah	Vater	fah-tah
e	eh / ay	entweder	ehnt-vay-dah
i	as in *itch* / ee	mit mir	mitt mee-ah
o	oh	oder	oh-dah
u	oo	unter	oon-tah
au	as in *out*	Maus	m-ou-ss
ai / ei	as in *eye*	ein	eye-n
ie	as in *me*	Miete	me-teh
eu	oy	heute	hoy-teh
äu	oy	häuten	hoy-ten
ß	ss	Fuß	fooss
g	as in *guy*	general	geh-neral
j	y	ja	ya
w	v	weiß	vice
v	f	viel	feel
s	z	See	zay
-r	ah	Mutter	moo-tah
In some regions *-er* is pronounced like an R with a tongue roll.			
ig	same as German *ich*	traurig	tr-ow-r*ich*
In some regions *-ig* is pronounced *-ick*			
qu	kv	quellen	kvellen
sch	sh	schnell	shnell
sp	shp	Spiel	shpeel
st-	sht	Stein	shtine
-st	st	Faust	foust
y	oo	Typ	toop
For words of English origin, the y is pronounced the same as English.			
z	ts	zu	tsu
th	t	Thema	tay-mah
tsch	ch	tschüs	chew-ss
tion	tsyon	Information	informa-tsyon
sion	zyon	Explosion	explo-zyon

A fun thing about German is that every letter is pronounced. There are no silent letters. This can be entertaining when you encounter words like *Pflanzen* (plants) and *Knie* (knee). Try practicing right now. Say *pf* and *kn*.

In linguistics, grouped vowel sounds are called diphthongs. *Ai, ei, ie, eu,* and *äu* are singular vowel sounds. You may find words with vowels next to each other which are not diphthongs, like *Boot* (boat) and *beeilen* (to hurry). The second *o* in *Boot* simply extends the sound. *Boot* has the same pronunciation as the English *boat*. Because *ei* is a diphthong, *beeilen* is pronounced beh-eye-len.

Commas are also a bit different in German. Unlike English, you can't just, throw a comma into any sentence, when you, want a pause. In German, commas are only used to separate clauses. Don't worry too much about it, just keep it in mind.

You Can Already Speak German

Many people say Spanish is very easy to speak because it is so similar to English. This is true, but German is even easier, because English is part of the Germanic language family. This family includes German, English, Swedish, Norwegian, and Dutch. Spanish is part of the Romance language family, which includes Spanish, French, Italian, and Latin.

German and English share an amazing number of cognates, that is, words that are the same or nearly the same in both languages. Let's look at some of these words.

Now that you know the basics of German pronunciation, try to pronounce all of the cognates:

accept akzeptieren
accent Akzent
acrobat Akrobat
active aktiv
acute akut
adapter Adapter
address Adresse
affair Affäre
agent Agent
alcohol Alkohol
all all
allergy Allergie
allegory Allegorie
alphabet Alphabet
altar Altar
amateur Amateur
analog analog
analysis Analyse
anarchy Anarchie
angel Engel
aquarium Aquarium
architect Architekt
army Armee
ash Asche
astronaut Astronaut
athlete Athlet
atlas Atlas
avocado Avocado
baby Baby
balcony Balkon
ball Ball
doctor Doktor
dolphin Delphin
dozen Dutzend
dream Traum

balloon Ballon
banana Banane
bank Bank
battery Batterie
bear Bär
bed Bett
beer Bier
bitter bitter
blind blind
blizzard Blizzard
blond(e) blond
blood Blut
blue blau
boat Boot
book Buch
boxer Boxer
bread Brot
broccoli Brokkoli
bus Bus
butter Butter
cabinet Kabinett
cable Kabel
café Café
calendar Kalender
calorie Kalorie
camel Kamel
camera Kamera
candidate Kandidat
cannibal Kannibale
cannon Kanone
caravan Karawane
father Vater
feather Feder
fever Fieber
fiasco Fiasko

card Karte
cardinal Kardinal
carrot Karotte
cassette Kassette
cat Katze
chocolate Schokolade
cigarette Zigarette
coffee Kaffee
coma Koma
compass Kompass
competent kompetent
complex komplex
complicated kompliziert
compromise Kompromiss
concert Konzert
continent Kontinent
cork Kork
creative kreativ
credit card Kreditkarte
critic Kritiker
crocodile Krokodil
curve Kurve
dance Tanz
date Datum
debut Debüt
decadent dekadent
diamond Diamant
discipline Disziplin
disco Disko
discussion Diskussion
dock Dock
guitar Gitarre
gymnastics Gymnastik
hair Haar
half halb

drink trinken	**figure** Figur	**hamburger** Hamburger
drug Droge	**film** Film	**hammer** Hammer
dumb dumm	**final** final	**hamster** Hamster
earnest ernst	**finance** Finanz	**hand** Hand
effective effektiv	**find** finden	**hang** hängen
ego Ego	**finger** Finger	**hard** hart
elbow Ellenbogen	**fish** Fisch	**hat** Hut
electricity Elektrizität	**fitness** Fitness	**helicopter** Helikopter
electronic elektronisch	**flag** Flagge	**here** hier
elegant elegant	**flame** Flamme	**hobby** Hobby
elephant Elefant	**form** Form	**homage** Hommage
emblem Emblem	**formal** formal	**horror** Horror
end Ende	**format** Format	**hotel** Hotel
energy Energie	**forum** Forum	**house** Haus
ethic Ethik	**fossil** Fossil	**humor** Humor
ethical ethisch	**fresh** frisch	**hundred** hundert
Europa Europa	**front** Front	**hunger** Hunger
exact exakt	**full** voll	**hygiene** Hygiene
exclusive exklusiv	**gallery** Galerie	**hypothesis** Hypothese
exist existieren	**gangster** Gangster	**hysteria** Hysterie
exotic exotisch	**garden** Garten	**ice** Eis
experiment Experiment	**generation** Generation	**idea** Idee
explosion Explosion	**genius** Genie	**ideal** ideal
fable Fabel	**gladiator** Gladiator	**identical** identisch
fabulous fabulös	**glamour** Glamour	**identity** Identität
fact Fakt	**glass** Glas	**ideology** Ideologie
faction Fraktion	**global** global	**idiot** Idiot
factor Faktor	**glossary** Glossar	**ignore** ignorieren
faculty Fakultät	**god** Gott	**illegal** illegal
fair fair	**gold** Gold	**illustrate** illustrieren
fall fallen	**golf** Golf	**imperialism** Imperialismus
false falsch	**grass** Gras	**import** importieren
family Familie	**gray** grau	**industry** Industrie
fan Fan	**green** grün	**information** Information
fantastic fantastisch	**grill** Grill	**insect** Insekt
fantasy Fantasie	**group** Gruppe	**intelligent** intelligent
farm Farm	**gum** Gummi	**jacket** Jacke
fascist Faschist	**guarantee** Garantie	**jaguar** Jaguar
fat Fett	**guaranteed** garantiert	**job** Job
journalist Journalist	**monarchy** Monarchie	**parasite** Parasit
kangaroo Känguru	**monster** Monster	**parade** Parade
kayak Kajak	**moon** Mond	**park** Park
ketchup Ketchup	**more** mehr	**parliament** Parlament
kilogram Kilogramm	**mother** Mutter	**parody** Parodie
kiss Kuss	**motor** Motor	**passenger** Passagier
knee Knie	**mouse** Maus	**password** Passwort
lamb Lamm	**mouth** Mund	**patent** Patent
lamp Lampe	**muscle** Muskel	**patient** Patient

lantern Laterne	**museum** Museum	**patriot** Patriot
learn lernen	**music** Musik	**pause** Pause
leather Leder	**myth** Mythos	**pedal** Pedal
liberal liberal	**name** Name	**pelican** Pelikan
license Lizenz	**nature** Natur	**pepper** Pfeffer
line Linie	**negative** negativ	**percent** Prozent
lip Lippe	**nephew** Neffe	**perfect** perfekt
list Liste	**nerve** Nerv	**perfume** Parfum
literature Literatur	**nest** Nest	**permanent** permanent
liver Leber	**net** Netz	**persistent** persistent
local lokal	**neutral** neutral	**person** Person
logic Logik	**new** neu	**perspective** Perspektive
lung Lunge	**nuclear** nuklear	**pessimist** Pessimist
machine Maschine	**number** Nummer	**philosophy** Philosophie
magic Magie	**obligation** Obligation	**photograph** Foto
magnet Magnet	**obsessive** obsessiv	**pill** Pille
man Mann	**officer** Offizier	**pirate** Pirat
manager Manager	**official** offiziell	**pizza** Pizza
margarine Margarine	**often** oft	**plan** Plan
market Markt	**oil** Öl	**planet** Planet
massage Massage	**omelet** Omelett	**plural** Plural
massive massiv	**opera** Oper	**poetry** Poesie
medicine Medizin	**optimal** optimal	**poker** Poker
melancholy Melancholie	**organ** Organ	**polar** polar
melody Melodie	**organization** Organisation	**pony** Pony
melon Melone	**oven** Ofen	**popular** populär
method Methode	**pair** Paar	**porcelain** Porzellan
mild mild	**palace** Palast	**portion** Portion
milk Milch	**pancreas** Pankreas	**post office** Post
mineral Mineral	**panda** Panda	**potent** potent
minute Minute	**pandemic** Pandemie	**pound** Pfund
mission Mission	**panic** Panik	**practical** praktisch
modern modern	**panorama** Panorama	**preposition** Präposition
moment Moment	**paper** Papier	**price** Preis
prime minister Premierminister	**radiator** Radiator	**senator** Senator
prince Prinz	**radio** Radio	**send** senden
private privat	**radius** Radius	**sensation** Sensation
product Produkt	**Sabbath** Sabbat	**sentimental** sentimental
profane profan	**sack** Sack	**sequence** Sequenz
professor Professor	**saga** Saga	**vacuum** Vakuum
profile Profil	**salad** Salat	**vampire** Vampir
profit Profit	**salt** Salz	**vandal** Vandale
program Programm	**sand** Sand	**vanilla** Vanille
project Projekt	**sarcasm** Sarkasmus	**vector** Vektorn
propaganda Propaganda	**satellite** Satellit	**vegetarian** vegetarisch
prose Prosa	**satire** Satire	**vein** Vene
puberty Pubertät	**sauna** Sauna	**verb** Verb
pulse Puls	**scandal** Skandal	**video** Video

qualification Qualifikation	**scene** Szene	**virus** Virus
quality Qualität	**sculpture** Skulptur	**visa** Visum
quantum Quantum	**sea** See	**vitamin** Vitamin
quiz Quiz	**second** Sekunde	**vocabulary** Vokabel
racist Rassist	**segment** Segment	**volcano** Vulkan
radar Radar	**seminar** Seminar	

Day 1: Question Words

Let's learn the basics, question words! Try these out on your friends today and watch for the funny looks on their faces as you speak German to them! Don't worry if you don't understand all of the grammar or vocabulary in the example sentences. For today, just memorize the vocabulary words.

<u>Day 1 Vocabulary</u>
1. **who** wer
2. **what** was
3. **where** wo
4. **when** wann
5. **why** warum / wieso
6. **how** wie
7. **where from** woher
8. **where to** wohin
9. **how much / how many** wie viel / wie viele
10. **there is / are** es gibt

<u>Example Sentences</u>
1. **Who are you?** Wer sind Sie?
2. **What is that?** Was ist das?
3. **Where am I?** Wo bin ich?
4. **When does it begin?** Wann fängt es an?
5. **Why are you doing that?** Warum machen Sie das?
6. **How are you?** Wie geht es Ihnen?
7. **Where are you from?** Woher kommen Sie?
8. **Where are you going?** Wohin gehen Sie?
9. **How many languages do you speak?** Wie viele Sprachen sprechen Sie?
10. **Is there more?** Gibt es noch mehr?

Day 2: Hello, Goodbye

Today let's practice a few greetings and farewells, so now you have something to say before your question words.

Day 2 Vocabulary
1. **Hello.** Hallo.
2. **Good morning.** Guten Morgen.
3. **Good day / afternoon.** Guten Tag.
4. **Good evening.** Guten Abend.
5. **Good night.** Gute Nacht.
6. **Goodbye.** Auf Wiedersehen.
7. **Bye.** Tschüss.
8. **See you soon.** Bis bald.
9. **See you then.** Bis dann.
10. **See you later.** Bis später.

Today there are no sentences to practice, so try combining these greetings and farewells with your question words from yesterday.

Day 3: Thank You

How is your studying going? Are you finding that you can remember the vocabulary words without looking at the cards? Try saying a few things right now. Feels good, doesn't it? Today let's learn a few more useful expressions. The focus today will be on *thank you* and *you're welcome*. You probably already know that *thank you* in German is *danke*. You're welcome is *bitte*. *Bitte* also means *please*. More words can be added to express our gratitude even more.

Thanks.	Danke.
Thanks a lot.	Danke sehr.
Thank you very much.	Danke schön.
You're welcome.	Bitte.
You're very welcome.	Bitte sehr.
You're very much welcome.	Bitte schön.

You'll notice, however, in English we don't really say things like *you're very much welcome*. The custom in German is just to use the same word the person used. For example, if someone says *danke schön* you answer *bitte schön*, and if someone says *danke sehr*, you answer *bitte sehr*.

Day 3 Vocabulary
1. **thanks** danke
2. **you're welcome / please** bitte
3. **very** sehr
4. **beautiful** schön
5. **Excuse me.** Entschuldigung.
6. **Pardon me?** Wie bitte?
7. **I'm sorry.** Es tut mir leid.
8. **Cheers! (drinking)** Prost!
9. **Good luck!** Viel Glück!
10. **Have fun!** Viel Spaß!

Day 4: Pronouns, To Be

Don't forget to quickly review what you practiced yesterday, go ahead and do that right now if you haven't already. Today's lesson will cover pronouns, some are very similar to English:

Pronouns			
I	ich	**we**	wir
you	du	**you all**	ihr
he	er	**they**	sie
she	sie	**you (formal)**	Sie
it	es		

There are a couple words here that don't have exact equivalents. *Ihr* is the plural form of *you*. In English we sometimes say *you all*. *Sie* is the formal or polite form of *you*. Use this when speaking with strangers, or to be extra polite. You may also notice that *sie* appears three times. That's right, *sie* means *she*, *they*, and *you*. But notice, the formal version is capitalized: *Sie*. In German, capitalization follows different rules. Every noun in German is capitalized, not just proper nouns as in English. Though only a pronoun, the polite form of *you* is also capitalized.

In German, the verb *to be* is *sein*. All verbs conjugate with the subject of the sentence. *Sein* is an irregular verb, so its conjugation follows special rules. Many other languages conjugate verbs as well, but we only do it to a limited degree in English. Take a look at this to help explain:

sein (to be)			
I am	ich bin	**we are**	wir sind
you are	du bist	**you all are**	ihr seid
he is	er ist	**they are**	sie sind
she is	sie ist	**you are (formal)**	Sie sind
it is	es ist		

Day 4 Vocabulary

You may wish to write the conjugations of *sein* next to each pronoun to help you remember them.
1. **I** ich
2. **you** du
3. **he** er
4. **she** sie
5. **it** es
6. **we** wir
7. **you all** ihr
8. **they** sie
9. **you (formal)** Sie
10. **to be** sein

Example Sentences
1. **I am Paul.** Ich bin Paul.
2. **You are nice.** Du bist nett.
3. **He is cute.** Er ist hübsch.
4. **She is beautiful.** Sie ist schön.
5. **It is ugly.** Es ist hässlich.
6. **We are nice.** Wir sind nett.
7. **You all are funny.** Ihr seid lustig.
8. **They are wonderful.** Sie sind wunderbar.
9. **(formal) You are American.** Sie sind Amerikaner.
10. **To be or not to be, that is the question.** Sein oder Nichtsein, das ist hier die Frage.

Day 5: Forming Questions, Nationalities

To form a question in German, simply switch the position of the noun and verb:

| **I am Paul.** | Ich bin Paul. |
| **Am I Paul?** | Bin ich Paul? |

Pretty easy right? Let's also learn how to say *yes* and *no*. *Yes* and *no* in German are *Ja* and *Nein* respectively. Today's vocabulary will be nationalities. Many nationalities will simply add the suffix *-er* to the country name. If you are female, the suffix becomes *-erin*. There are many exceptions to this rule, and the German nationality is one of them. These words are nouns: *Deutscher* literally means, *a German person*. When you say *Ich bin Deutscher*, you are literally saying *I am a German person*, but the translation is *I am German*.

This lesson will introduce Grammar Cards. Study them like you do your vocabulary cards, and be sure to include an example sentence on each Grammar Card.

Day 5 Grammar Card
1. **Male person**
Add suffix *-er*
2. **Female person**
Add suffix *-erin.*

Day 5 Vocabulary
1. **Australian** Australier / Australierin
2. **German** Deutscher / Deutsche
3. **American** Amerikaner / Amerikanerin
4. **French** Franzose / Französin
5. **Spanish** Spanier / Spanierin
6. **Italian** Italiener / Italienerin
7. **British** Brite / Britin
8. **Swiss** Schweizer / Schweizerin
9. **Japanese** Japaner / Japanerin
10. **Chinese** Chinese / Chinesin (pronounced key-naze / key-naze-in)

Example Sentences
1. **Am I Australian?** Bin ich Australier? / Bin ich Australierin?
2. **You are German.** Du bist Deutscher. / Du bist Deutsche.
3. **Is he American?** Ist er Amerikaner?
4. **Is she French?** Ist sie Französin?
5. **No, she is Spanish.** Nein, sie ist Spanierin.
6. **Are you Italian?** Sind Sie Italiener? / Sind Sie Italienerin?
7. **Are you British?** Sind Sie Brite? / Sind Sie Britin?
8. **I am Swiss.** Ich bin Schweizer. / Ich bin Schweizerin.
9. **Are you Japanese?** Sind Sie Japaner? / Sind Sie Japanerin?
10. **She is Chinese.** Sie ist Chinesin.

Day 6: Noun Gender, Plural Nouns

Today's lesson covers the definite articles, *the* and *that*. In German, all nouns have a gender: masculine, feminine, or neutral. There are three ways to say *the*:

Definite Articles	
Masculine	der
Feminine	die
Neutral	das
Plural	die

Remembering the gender of nouns is very important in German, it is essential later for grammar. Every time you memorize a noun, you need to also remember the gender.

There are many different ways to pluralize words in German. Plural words can add an *-e, -en,* or *-er*, as well as cause a vowel change. Some words have the same singular and plural form. Some foreign loaned words use an *-s* like in English. Study the following examples:

No change	Add -er
the window / the windows das Fenster / die Fenster	**the child / the children** das Kind / die Kinder
Add -e	Add -er, vowel change
the table / the tables der Tisch / die Tische	**the book / the books** das Buch / die Bücher
Add -en	Add -s
the door / the doors die Tür / die Türen	**the camera / the cameras** die Kamera / die Kameras

This is a lot of information to absorb at once, but don't worry. Memorizing the plural form of nouns is not really all that important. As you continue to practice and use your German it will become easier and easier to remember the gender and plural forms of nouns. But don't be afraid to make mistakes, even if you completely forget the gender of a noun a German speaker will still be able to understand what you are saying, and that is what is most important: being understood, communicating ideas.

That translates to *das*. Today, look around your room and ask yourself this question: *Was ist das*? (What is that?) You answer will be: *Das ist ~*. Don't forget, all nouns in German are capitalized.

The plural forms of nouns will be noted with parenthesis. If there are no parenthesis, the plural form is the same as the singular form. The first letter will show if there is a vowel change, and the second will be the ending. Study the following example:

chair der Stuhl (ü, -e)
The plural form of chair is *Stühle*.

Day 6 Vocabulary
1. **table / desk** der Tisch (-e)
2. **wall** die Wand (ä, -e)
3. **window** das Fenster
4. **chair** der Stuhl (ü, -e)
5. **door** die Tür (-en)
6. **bed** das Bett (-en)
7. **floor** der Boden (ö)
8. **lamp** die Lampe (-n)
9. **pillow** das Kissen
10. **TV** der Fernseher

Example Sentences
1. **The table is big.** Der Tisch ist groß.
2. **The wall is white.** Die Wand ist weiß.
3. **The window is dirty.** Das Fenster ist schmutzig.
4. **The chair is small.** Der Stuhl ist klein.
5. **The door is narrow.** Die Tür ist eng.
6. **The bed is wide.** Das Bett ist breit.
7. **The floor is clean.** Der Boden ist sauber.
8. **The lamp is bright.** Die Lampe ist hell.
9. **The pillow is soft.** Das Kissen ist weich.
10. **The TV is broken.** Der Fernseher ist kaputt.

Day 7: A, An, Not

Today's lesson covers the indefinite article *a*. *A* in German is *ein* for masculine and neutral nouns, and *eine* for feminine nouns.

Not in German is *nicht*. Where to place *nicht* in a sentence can be a bit tricky, but the basic rule is to place it before the word you want to negate.

I am not Paul.	Ich bin nicht Paul. (negates *Paul*)

There a few other rules about moving *nicht* to the end of a sentence, or putting it somewhere else, but the rules are rather useless to memorize. Just remember the basic rule of putting it before the word you want to negate. As you practice and speak with native speakers, it will become natural for you to know where you put *nicht*. Again, even if you make a mistake, the listener will still understand you, so don't be afraid.

Nicht + ein / nicht eine (not a) become *kein / keine*. Study the following examples:

I am not a pillow.	Ich bin kein Kissen.
I am not a door.	Ich bin keine Tür.

Nothing in German is *nichts*. Some people write and pronounce this as *nix*. Try not to confuse *nicht* and *nichts*.   Today, practice again by asking yourself: *Was ist das?* But this time, use *a* and *not*. For example:

What is that?	Was ist das?
That is a table.	Das ist ein Tisch.
Is that a wall?	Ist das eine Wand?
No, that is not a wall.	Nein, das ist keine Wand.

<u>Day 7 Grammar Cards</u>
1. **nicht + ein / eine**
kein / keine
2. **nothing**
nichts

<u>Day 7 Vocabulary</u>
1. **man / husband** der Mann (ä, -er)
2. **woman / wife** die Frau (-en)
3. **child** das Kind (-er)
4. **brother** der Bruder (ü)
5. **sister** die Schwester (-n)
6. **father** der Vater (ä)
7. **mother** die Mutter (ü)
8. **uncle** der Onkel
9. **aunt** die Tante (-n)
10. **siblings** die Geschwister

<u>Example Sentences</u>
1. **Are you a man?** Sind Sie ein Mann?
2. **I am not a woman.** Ich bin keine Frau.
3. **She is a child.** Sie ist ein Kind.
4. **He is a brother.** Er ist ein Bruder.
5. **She is a sister.** Sie ist eine Schwester.
6. **He is not a father.** Er ist kein Vater.
7. **She is not a mother.** Sie ist keine Mutter.
8. **He is not an uncle.** Er ist kein Onkel.
9. **She is not an aunt.** Sie ist keine Tante.
10. **We are not siblings.** Wir sind keine Geschwister.

Day 8: Accusative Case

There are four grammatical structures in German: nominative, accusative, dative, and genitive. Nominative marks the subject of a verb, accusative marks the object, dative marks the indirect object, and genitive shows ownership. So far, all of the example sentences have only had the nominative case.

Masculine nouns change in the accusative case. Feminine, neutral, and plural nouns do not change. Study the following changes:

Nominative	der	ein	kein
Accusative	den	einen	keinen

The Accusative case is used for direct objects. Sentences using verbs that show existence or a change in state, such as *sein* (to be) and *werden* (to become) will always be nominative, because they are not objects of the verb. Study the following examples:

The TV is broken.	Der Fernseher ist kaputt.
A TV is broken.	Ein Fernseher ist kaputt.
I have the TV.	Ich habe den Fernseher.
I have a TV.	Ich habe einen Fernseher.

Verbs conjugation will be covered in detail later in the book, but for now, study the conjugation of *haben* (to have) so that you can practice today's example sentences with the accusative case. Instead of the two syllable *habe*, many Germans will say the one syllable unvoiced version of *habe*, which sounds like *hap*.

haben (to have)	
ich habe	wir haben
du hast	ihr habt
er hat	sie haben
sie hat	Sie haben
es hat	

Day 8 Grammar Card

Nominative	der	ein	kein
Accusative	den	einen	keinen

Day 8 Vocabulary
1. **head** der Kopf (ö, -e)
2. **eye** das Auge (-n)
3. **ear** das Ohr (-en)
4. **nose** die Nase (-n)
5. **mouth** der Mund (ü, -er)
6. **face** das Gesicht (-er)
7. **neck** der Hals (ä, -e)
8. **arm** der Arm (-e)
9. **hand** die Hand (ä, -e)
10. **finger** der Finger

Example Sentences
1. **I have a head.** Ich habe einen Kopf.
2. **You have an eye.** Du hast ein Auge.
3. **She has the ear.** Sie hat das Ohr.
4. **We have the nose.** Wir haben die Nase.
5. **You all have a mouth.** Ihr habt einen Mund.
6. **They have the face.** Sie haben das Gesicht.
7. **You have a neck.** Sie haben einen Hals.
8. **I have the arm.** Ich habe den Arm.
9. **He has a hand.** Er hat eine Hand.
10. **It has a finger.** Es hat einen Finger.

Day 9: Accusative Pronouns

Pronouns will also take the accusative case as direct objects. Certain verbs and prepositions also force you to use the accusative case. Prepositions will be covered later, but many of today's example sentences will use the preposition für (for), which always takes the accusative case. Study the following changes:

Accusative Pronouns	
ich → mich	wir → uns
du → dich	ihr → euch
er → ihn	sie (no change)
sie (no change)	Sie (no change)
es (no change)	

Day 9 Grammar Card

Accusative Pronouns	
mich	uns
dich	euch
ihn	sie
sie	Sie
es	

Day 9 Vocabulary
1. **meat** das Fleisch
2. **breakfast** das Frühstück (-e)
3. **lunch** das Mittagessen
4. **dinner** das Abendessen
5. **chicken** das Huhn (ü, -er)
6. **egg** das Ei (-er)
7. **milk** die Milch
8. **potato** die Kartoffel (-n)
9. **water** das Wasser
10. **juice** der Saft (ä, -e)

Example Sentences
1. **Is that meat for me?** Ist das Fleisch für mich?
2. **That breakfast is for you.** Das Frühstück ist für dich.
3. **I have no lunch for him.** Ich habe kein Mittagessen für ihn.
4. **She has dinner for her.** Sie hat Abendessen für sie.
5. **That is for the chicken.** Das ist für das Huhn.
6. **Do you have eggs for us?** Haben Sie Eier für uns?
7. **The milk is for you all.** Der Milch ist für euch.
8. **The potatoes are for you.** Die Kartoffeln sind für Sie.
9. **You should drink water.** Du solltest Wasser trinken.
10. **I don't like juice.** Ich mag Saft nicht.

Day 10: Possessives

Today's lesson covers possessives. Study the following possessive pronouns:

Possessives	
ich → mein	wir → unser
du → dein	ihr → euer
er → sein	sie → ihr
sie → ihr	Sie → Ihr
es → sein	

Notice that *sein* (his) and *sein* (its) is the same word as *sein* (to be). Notice also that *sie*, *sie*, and *Sie* use the same word as *you all* (ihr). This isn't a typo, the words are homonyms, so be careful! One final note, when conjugating *euer*, the final *e* and *r* will switch places: *eure, euren.*

Possessives must be conjugated as well. The conjugation rules are the same as the conjugation for *ein.* Study the following example:

I have a TV.	Ich habe ein<u>en</u> Fernseher.
I have your TV.	Ich habe dein<u>en</u> Fernseher.

Day 10 Grammar Card

Possessives	
mein	unser
dein	euer
sein	ihr
ihr	Ihr
sein	

Day 10 Vocabulary
1. **hat** der Hut (ü, -e)
2. **shirt** das Hemd (-en)
3. **dress** das Kleid (-er)
4. **clothing / clothes** die Kleidung / die Kleider
5. **pants** die Hose (-n)
6. **skirt** der Rock (ö, -e)
7. **shoe** der Schuh (-e)
8. **suit** der Anzug (ü, -e)
9. **belt** der Gürtel
10. **coat** der Mantel (ä)

Example Sentences
1. **That is my hat.** Das ist mein Hut.
2. **Do you have your shirt?** Hast du dein Hemd?
3. **She is wearing her dress.** Sie trägt ihr Kleid.
4. **He has our clothes.** Er hat unsere Kleidung / Kleider.
5. **She has his pants.** Sie hat seine Hose.
6. **Are you all wearing your skirts?** Tragt ihr eure Röcke?
7. **We have our shoes.** Wir haben unsere Schuhe.
8. **Do you have your suit?** Haben Sie Ihren Anzug?
9. **They have their belts.** Sie haben ihre Gürtel.
10. **I am wearing his coat.** Ich trage seinen Mantel.

Day 11: Dative Case

The dative case is used for indirect objects. It indicates *to whom* or *for whom* something happens. For example, the sentence: *I gave the flowers to my mother. Mother* is the indirect object. The dative case has its own conjugation. Study the following changes:

Dative Articles	
der → dem	ein → einem
die → der	eine → einer
das → dem	ein → einem
die (plural) → den	keine (plural) → keinen

Now that you have learned three of the cases, it's time to introduce a grammar table, which can help you visualize the changes:

Definite Articles				
	Masculine	Feminine	Neutral	Plural
Nominative	der	die	das	die
Accusative	den	die	das	die
Dative	dem	der	dem	den

Indefinite Articles				
	Masculine	Feminine	Neutral	Plural
Nominative	ein	eine	ein	keine
Accusative	einen	eine	ein	keine
Dative	einem	einer	einem	keinen

Note the plural form of *ein* is always negative because you can't say *A people* but you can say *No people*.

	Dative Articles			
	Masculine	Feminine	Neutral	Plural
Definite	dem	der	dem	den
Indefinite	einem	einer	einem	einen

Day 11 Vocabulary
1. **refrigerator** der Kühlschrank (ä, -e)
2. **microwave** die Mikrowelle (-n)
3. **oven** der Ofen (ö)
4. **stove** der Herd (-e)
5. **carpet/rug** der Teppich (-e)
6. **fork** die Gabel (-n)
7. **spoon** der Löffel
8. **knife** das Messer
9. **napkin** die Serviette (-n)
10. **plate** der Teller

Example Sentences
1. **We are buying the man a refrigerator.** Wir kaufen dem Mann einen Kühlschrank.
2. **I am giving my mother a microwave.** Ich gebe meiner Mutter eine Mikrowelle.
3. **He is buying an oven for his father.** Er kauft seinem Vater einen Ofen.
4. **Can you clean the stove for your mom?** Kannst du deiner Mutter den Herd putzen?
5. **She is giving the child a rug.** Sie gibt dem Kind einen Teppich.
6. **They are giving their guests the forks.** Sie geben ihren Gästen die Gabeln.
7. **She is sending her mother a spoon.** Sie schickt ihrer Mutter einen Löffel.
8. **I am buying a friend a knife.** Ich kaufe einem Freund ein Messer.
9. **You all should give your guests napkins.** Ihr solltet euren Gästen Servietten geben.
10. **Can you buy my brother this plate?** Kannst du meinem Bruder diesen Teller kaufen?

Day 12: Dative Pronouns

Dative pronouns are just as important as accusative pronouns, and you will use them a lot. Again, the dative case marks the indirect object, it indicates *to whom* or *for whom* something happens. Study the following changes:

Dative Pronouns	
ich → mir	wir → uns
du → dir	ihr → euch
er → ihm	sie → ihnen
sie → ihr	Sie → Ihnen
es → ihm	

Study the following example:

He gives me flowers.	Er gibt mir Blumen.

Review all of the pronouns with the following grammar table:

Pronouns				
	Nominative	Accusative	Dative	Possessive
I	ich	mich	mir	mein
you	du	dich	dir	dein
he	er	ihn	ihm	sein
she	sie	sie	ihr	ihr
it	es	es	ihm	sein
we	wir	uns	uns	unser
you all	ihr	euch	euch	euer
they	sie	sie	ihnen	ihr
you (formal)	Sie	Sie	Ihnen	Ihr

Many common set phrases dealing with your feelings use dative pronouns. The most important being *How are you?* and *I'm sorry*. Many of these phrases use the verb *tun* (to do), literally saying that something *does* (adjective) *to you*. Study the following examples:

How are you?	Wie geht es Ihnen.	Lit. How goes it for you?
I'm sorry.	Es tut mir leid.	Lit. That does sorrow to me.
That hurts me.	Das tut mir weh.	Lit. That does pain to me.
That's good for me.	Das tut mir gut.	Lit. That does good to me.
I enjoy that.	Das macht mir Spaß.	Lit. That does fun to me.
I am cold.	Mir ist kalt.	Lit. It is cold for me.

Day 12 Grammar Card

Dative Pronouns	
mir	uns
dir	euch
ihm	ihnen
ihr	Ihnen
ihm	

There are a couple verbs in today's vocabulary. Verbs will be explained in great detail later. For now just write them on your cards.

Day 12 Vocabulary
1. **example** das Beispiel (-e)
2. **country** das Land (ä, -er)
3. **world** die Welt (-en)
4. **reason** der Grund (ü, -e)
5. **money** das Geld (-er)
6. **thing (tangible only)** das Ding (-e)
7. **thing (tangible or intangible)** die Sache (-n)
8. **to hurt** weh'tun |tat weh, wehgetan|
9. **to be sorry / cause sorrow** leid'tun |tat leid, leidgetan|
10. **fun** der Spaß

Example Sentences
1. **Can you give me an example?** Kannst du mir ein Beispiel geben?
2. **The country gives them welfare.** Das Land gibt ihnen Sozialhilfe.
3. **I am showing you the world.** Ich zeige dir die Welt.
4. **Shall I give you a reason?** Soll ich Ihnen einen Grund geben?
5. **Can you all give me some money?** Könnt ihr mir etwas Geld geben?
6. **He is giving her that thing.** Er gibt ihr das Ding.
7. **I buy many things for you.** Ich kaufe dir viele Sachen.
8. **You are hurting me.** Du tust mir weh.
9. **I pity you.** Du tust mir leid. (Lit. You cause me sorrow.)
10. **German is fun!** Deutsch macht mir Spaß!

Day 13: Der Words

Der words are certain words that also require conjugation. When you use these words, you must add the appropriate ending, which are similar to the *der / die / das* endings, hence the name: *Der words*. Study the following list and grammar table:

Der Word Stems	
all / every	all-
this	dies-
each / every	jed-
that (far away)	jen-
some / many	manch-
such	solch-
which	welch-

Der Word Endings				
	Masculine	Feminine	Neutral	Plural
Nominative	-er	-e	-es	-e
Accusative	-en	-e	-es	-e
Dative	-em	-er	-em	-en

Study the following examples:

Masculine Nominative	
This man is fat.	Dieser Mann ist dick.
Plural Accusative	
I hate such people.	Ich hasse solche Leute.
Masculine Accusative	
She is eating every pancake!	Sie isst jeden Pfannkuchen!

Wer (who) is also a Der word, but it is bit special because it can only exist in the masculine form. The three forms are *wer* (nominative) *wen* (accusative) and *wem* (dative).

Der Word Endings				
	Masculine	Feminine	Neutral	Plural
Nominative	-er	-e	-es	-e
Accusative	-en	-e	-es	-e
Dative	-em	-er	-em	-en

2. **wer (accusative) / wer (dative)**
wen / wem

Day 13 Vocabulary
1. **all / every** all-
2. **this** dies-
3. **each / every** jed-
4. **that (far away)** jen-
5. **some / many** manch-
6. **such** solch-
7. **which** welch-
8. **person** die Person (-en)
Die Person is not used very commonly in German, it is used mostly for the intangible idea of personhood, rather than a physical body. *Die Leute* and *der Mensch* are much more common for saying *people* and *the person*. *Die Person* has a different feeling than in English, this can be illustrated in the phrase *pro Person*, which means *per capita*, or *per person*.
9. **people** die Leute
10. **human / person** der Mensch (-en)

Example Sentences
1. **I want everything!** Ich will alles!
2. **This man is fat.** Dieser Mann ist dick.
3. **She is eating every pancake!** Sie isst jeden Pfannkuchen!
4. **Do you know that man way over there?** Kennst du jenen Mann?
5. **Some people are very nice.** Manche Leute sind sehr nett.
6. **I hate such people.** Ich hasse solche Leute.
7. **Which movie are they seeing?** Welchen Film sehen sie?
8. **It costs 100 Euros per person.** Es kostet 100 Euro pro Person.
9. **German people are blunt.** Deutsche Leute sind direkt.
10. **Humans are inherently good.** Menschen sind von Natur aus gut.

Day 14: Genitive Case

The genitive case shows ownership. However, it is rarely used in spoken German. To show ownership in English, an apostrophe and S is used. In German, you can also simply add -s to show ownership, no apostrophe is necessary. However, this can only be used for proper nouns. Study the following examples:

Peter's house is big.	Peters Haus ist groß.
David's bed is small.	Davids Bett ist klein.

For all other nouns, the genitive case is used. Think of it as adding *of* to the article. Study the following list:

Genitive Articles	
der → des	ein → eines
die → der	eine → einer
das → des	ein → eines
die (plural) → der	keine (plural) → keiner

The grammar tables are now complete. Review the articles:

Definite Articles				
	Masculine	Feminine	Neutral	Plural
Nominative	der	die	das	die
Accusative	den	die	das	die
Dative	dem	der	dem	den
Genitive	des	der	des	der

Indefinite Articles				
	Masculine	Feminine	Neutral	Plural
Nominative	ein	eine	ein	keine
Accusative	einen	eine	ein	keine
Dative	einem	einer	einem	keinen
Genitive	eines	einer	eines	keiner

When using the genitive case with masculine and neutral nouns, -es / -s must also be added to the end of the owner. Most one syllable nouns take -es instead of -s. Study the following examples:

| My father's house is big. | Das Haus mein<u>es</u> Vater<u>s</u> ist groß. | Lit. The house of my father is big. |
| Her brother's bed is small. | Das Bett ih<u>res</u> Bruder<u>s</u> ist klein. | Lit. The bed of her brother is small. |

Again, in spoken German, the genitive case is not very popular. It's going out of style. More often, people will simply use the dative case instead with the preposition *von* (of). Study the following sentences with the dative case:

| My father's house is big. | Das Haus von meinem Vater ist groß. |
| Her brother's bed is small. | Das Bett von ihrem Bruder ist klein. |

Day 14 Grammar Card

Genitive Articles		
	Definite	Indefinite
Masculine	des + -es / -s	eines + -es / -s
Feminine	der	einer
Neutral	des + -es / -s	eines + -es / -s
Plural	der	keiner

Day 14 Vocabulary
1. **garden** der Garten (ä)
2. **flower** die Blume (-n)
3. **tree** der Baum (ä, -e)
4. **lawn** der Rasen
5. **to plant** pflanzen
6. **mountain / hill** der Berg (-e)
7. **beach** der Strand (ä, -e)
8. **to hike** wandern
9. **to swim** schwimmen |schwamm, geschwommen|
10. **ocean** das Meer (-e)

Example Sentences
1. **My mother's garden is beautiful.** Der Garten meiner Mutter ist schön.
2. **The city's flower is a rose.** Die Blume der Stadt ist eine Rose.
3. **The trees of the forest are huge.** Die Bäume des Waldes sind riesig.
4. **My friend's lawn is green.** Der Rasen meines Freundes ist grün.
5. **I like to plant flowers in my garden.** Ich pflanze gern Blumen in meinem Garten.
6. **The mountains of Switzerland are great.** Die Berge der Schweiz sind toll.
7. **Hawaii's beaches are white.** Hawaiis Strände sind weiß.
8. **Do you want to go hiking?** Willst du wandern gehen?
9. **They are swimming in the sea.** Sie schwimmen im Meer.
10. **The oceans of the world are vast.** Die Meere der Welt sind weit.

Day 15: Noun Practice

You've now learned all of the basics of nouns. The next few lessons will just be vocabulary. Use these lessons and the new nouns to practice all of the grammar you have studied in the last two weeks.

Day 15 Vocabulary
1. **house** das Haus (ä, -er)
2. **apartment** die Wohnung (-en)
3. **room** das Zimmer
4. **kitchen** die Küche (-n)
5. **bathroom** das Badezimmer
6. **entrance** der Eingang (ä, -e)
7. **bedroom** das Schlafzimmer
8. **living room** das Wohnzimmer
9. **roof** das Dach (ä, -er)
10. **cover / ceiling / blanket** die Decke (-n)

Example Sentences
1. **Is that a house?** Ist das ein Haus?
2. **That is not an apartment.** Das ist keine Wohnung.
3. **The room is beautiful.** Das Zimmer ist schön.
4. **The kitchen is ugly.** Die Küche ist hässlich.
5. **The bathroom is cold.** Das Badezimmer ist kalt.
6. **Where is the entrance?** Wo ist der Eingang?
7. **Where is the bedroom?** Wo ist das Schlafzimmer?
8. **There is no living room.** Es gibt kein Wohnzimmer.
9. **The roof is broken.** Das Dach ist kaputt.
10. **That is the ceiling.** Das ist die Decke.

Day 16: Noun Practice

<u>Day 16 Vocabulary</u>
1. **goal** das Ziel (-e)
2. **business / store** das Geschäft (-e)
3. **trash / garbage / rubbish** der Müll
4. **prison / jail** das Gefängnis (-se)
5. **safety / security / guarantee** die Sicherheit (-en)
6. **freedom / liberty** die Freiheit (-en)
7. **picture / drawing** das Bild (-er)
8. **sense / meaning** der Sinn (-e)
9. **air** die Luft (ü, -e)
10. **weapon** die Waffe (-n)

<u>Example Sentences</u>
1. **I would choose a new goal.** Ich würde ein neues Ziel auswählen.
2. **The business opens very early.** Das Geschäft öffnet sehr früh.
3. **Can you throw the trash out?** Kannst du den Müll wegwerfen.
4. **If I did that, I would go to jail.** Wenn ich das tun würde, müsste ich ins Gefängnis.
5. **Safety is very important.** Sicherheit ist sehr wichtig.
6. **Freedom is not free.** Freiheit hat ihren Preis.
7. **His drawing was very beautiful.** Sein Bild war sehr schön.
8. **This sentence makes no sense.** Dieser Satz ergibt keinen Sinn.
9. **The air is very cold in Germany.** Die Luft ist sehr kalt in Deutschland.
10. **I wouldn't use a weapon.** Ich würde keine Waffe benutzen.

Day 17: Noun Practice

Day 17 Vocabulary
1. **view / glance** der Blick (-e)
2. **place / room / space** der Platz (ä, -e)
3. **street** die Straße (-n)
4. **town** der Ort (-e)
5. **city** die Stadt (ä, -e)
6. **piece** das Stück (-e)
Stück does not require the preposition *of* like in English. For example: *ein Stück Schokolade* (a piece of chocolate). Also, the conjugation is based on the the neutral noun *Stück*. It doesn't matter if the piece of something is masculine, feminine, or neutral.
7. **fear** die Angst (ä, -e)
Angst is most often used to say you are afraid of something, by combining it with *haben*. The preposition used is *vor*.
8. **art** die Kunst (ü, -e)
9. **job / career** der Beruf (-e)
*To ask about someone's job say: *Was sind Sie von Beruf?* (Lit. What are you of job?) To answer simply say *Ich bin...(I am ...)*.
10. **sentence** der Satz (ä, -e)

Example Sentences
1. **It was love at first sight.** Es war Liebe auf den ersten Blick.
2. **Do you have a place for me?** Hast du einen Platz für mich?
3. **The streets have no names.** Die Straßen haben keine Namen.
4. **The town is very scenic.** Der Ort ist malerisch.
5. **Some cities are very crowded.** Manche Städte sind sehr überfüllt.
6. **Can you give me a piece of chocolate?** Kannst du mir ein Stück Schokolade geben?
7. **Are you afraid of bears?** Haben Sie Angst vor Bären?
8. **They can't understand his art.** Sie können seine Kunst nicht verstehen.
9. **What do you do? (job)** Was sind Sie von Beruf?
10. **This sentence is too long.** Dieser Satz ist zu lang.

Day 18: Noun Practice

Day 18 Vocabulary
1. **sky / heaven** der Himmel
2. **sun** die Sonne (-n)
3. **star** der Stern (-e)
4. **cloud** die Wolke (-n)
5. **weather** das Wetter
6. **snow** der Schnee
7. **fog** der Nebel
8. **windy** windig
9. **cloudy** bewölkt
10. **space / the Universe** das Weltall

Example Sentences
1. **The sky is beautiful today.** Der Himmel ist schön heute.
2. **The sun is shining!** Die Sonne scheint!
3. **There are many stars in the sky.** Es gibt viele Sterne am Himmel.
4. **The clouds are gray.** Die Wolken sind grau.
5. **How's the weather today?** Wie ist das Wetter heute?
6. **Do you like the snow?** Gefällt dir der Schnee?
7. **The fog is thick.** Der Nebel ist dick.
8. **It is really windy.** Es ist sehr windig.
9. **Germany is always cloudy.** Deutschland ist immer bewölkt.
10. **The Universe has many galaxies.** Das Weltall hat viele Galaxien.

Day 19: Noun Practice

<u>Day 19 Vocabulary</u>
1. **airport** der Flughafen (ä)
2. **city hall** das Rathaus (ä, -er)
3. **castle** das Schloss (ö, -er)
4. **school** die Schule (-n)
5. **bar** die Kneipe (-n)
6. **village** das Dorf (ö, -er)
7. **cemetery** der Friedhof (ö, -e)
8. **subway** die U-Bahn (-en)
9. **train** der Zug (ü, -e)
10. **car** der Wagen / das Auto (-s)
*There are two words for *car*, *Auto* and *Wagen*. What is the difference? It's largely up to the speaker. *Auto* can only refer to cars, not semi-trucks or extremely large vehicles. A *Wagen* can be almost anything with wheels.

<u>Example Sentences</u>
1. **I went to the airport yesterday.** Gestern bin ich zum Flughafen gefahren.
2. **Where is city hall?** Wo ist das Rathaus?
3. **Germany has many castles.** Deutschland hat viele Schlösser.
4. **How long did you go to school?** Wie lange bist du zur Schule gegangen?
5. **Let's go to a bar.** Lass uns in eine Kneipe gehen.
6. **My hometown is a small village.** Meine Heimatstadt ist ein kleines Dorf.
7. **That's not a park, but a cemetery.** Das ist kein Park, sondern ein Friedhof.
8. **I am taking the subway.** Ich nehme die U-Bahn.
9. **The train is late.** Der Zug hat Verspätung.
10. **I'll go by car.** Ich fahre mit dem Auto.

Day 20: Present Tense

Present tense verbs in German have three meanings: *I ~, I am ~ing, I do ~*. There is no separate grammar for the continuous tense. All verbs in German except *sein* (to be) and *tun* (to do) end with -*en*. There are two types of verbs in German, called strong verbs and weak verbs. In English we say irregular and regular verbs. To conjugate any verb, drop the final -*en* and add the following ending:

Present Tense Conjugation			
ich	-e	wir	-en
du	-st	ihr	-t
er	-t	sie	-en
sie	-t	Sie	-en
es	-t		

Notice for *wir*, *sie*, and *Sie* there is no real change because -*en* is added right back. Study the following verb conjugation:

sagen (to say)			
ich	sage	wir	sagen
du	sagst	ihr	sagt
er	sagt	sie	sagen
sie	sagt	Sie	sagen
es	sagt		

If a verb ends with -*ten* like *arbeiten* (to work), only drop the -*n* in the *du*, *ihr*, and *er / sie / es* forms. This makes sense, because it's kind of difficult to say something like *Du arbeitst*. Study the following example:

arbeiten (to work)			
ich	arbeite	wir	arbeiten
du	arbeit**est**	ihr	arbeitet
er	arbeit**et**	sie	arbeiten
sie	arbeit**et**	Sie	arbeiten
es	arbeit**et**		

To practice verb conjugation, ask yourself often: *Was mache ich?* (What am I doing?). Answer out loud.

Present Tense Conjugation			
ich	-e	wir	-en
du	-st	ihr	-t
er	-t	sie	-en
sie	-t	Sie	-en
es	-t		

One difficult thing about German is using the correct preposition. Today you will learn the word *fragen* (to ask). In American English we say *ask about*. The German word for *about* is *über*. But Germans don't use *über* with *fragen,* they use *nach* (after). If you want to *ask about* something, say *fragen nach*, which literally means *ask after*. Unfortunately, many verbs in German use prepositions that are different than English, and you just have to memorize them, so make a note on your card to use *nach*. Prepositions will be covered in detail in later lessons.

Day 20 Vocabulary
1. **to say** sagen
2. **to hear** hören
3. **to do / to make** machen
4. **to work** arbeiten
5. **to ask / question** fragen *nach*
6. **to study / to learn** lernen
7. **to talk** reden
8. **to buy** kaufen
9. **to love** lieben
10. **to play** spielen

Example Sentences
1. **What is she saying?** Was sagt sie?
2. **Do you hear that?** Hörst du das?
3. **What are you doing?** Was machen Sie?
4. **Where do you work?** Wo arbeitest du?
5. **We are asking her about something.** Wir fragen sie nach etwas.
6. **I study every day.** Ich lerne jeden Tag.
7. **They are always talking.** Sie reden immer.
8. **I buy milk at the supermarket.** Ich kaufe Milch im Supermarkt.
9. **Do you love me?** Liebst du mich?
10. **The kids play every day.** Die Kinder spielen jeden Tag.

Day 21: Strong and Weak Verbs

Strong (irregular) verbs have a different past tense conjugation than weak verbs, and a lot of them also change their vowel in the present tense for the *du* and *er / sie / es* form. A few weak verbs are also irregular, and will be noted in the vocabulary section. Study the following conjugation:

sehen (to see)			
ich	sehe	wir	sehen
du	siehst	ihr	seht
er	sieht	sie	sehen
sie	sieht	Sie	sehen
es	sieht		

Do you see how the *e* changes to *ie* in the *du* and *er / sie / es* forms? Most strong verbs have a vowel change like this. It may be tough now, but it will actually become very easy once you memorize a few verbs. You will eventually be able to tell if a verb has a vowel change even if it is the first time you see it!

Another strong verb is *essen* (to eat). Not only does *essen* have a vowel change, but the *du* form is the same as the *er / sie / es* form. This is because *issst* with three S's would look strange. Study the following conjugation:

essen (to eat)			
ich	esse	wir	essen
du	isst	ihr	esst
er	isst	sie	essen
sie	isst	Sie	essen
es	isst		

Strong verbs will have the following format in the vocabulary sections:

infinite (3rd person form) |simple past, past participle|

The simple past and past participle will be covered later, but write them on your note cards for now. Some verbs will also have a preposition associated with them, which differs from the prepositions we use in English. These will be written in *italics*.

Day 21 Vocabulary
1. **to go / walk / to work** gehen |ging, gegangen|
*To work here means *to be in working order* or *to function*.
2. **to see** sehen (sieht) |sah, gesehen|
3. **to come** kommen |kam, gekommen|
4. **to eat** essen (isst) |aß, gegessen|
5. **to drink** trinken |trank, getrunken|
6. **to think *of / about*** denken *an* |dachte, gedacht|
7. **to sing** singen |sang, gesungen|
8. **to speak** sprechen (spricht) |sprach, gesprochen|
9. **to write** schreiben |schrieb, geschrieben|
10. **to drive / to go** fahren (fährt) |fuhr, gefahren|
Fahren can also be translated as *to go*. English uses the verb *to go* without ever indicating the method. Are we driving there? Are we flying? In German, however, they will most always use the verb that shows the method by which they are going.

Example Sentences
1. **Where are you going?** Wohin gehen Sie?
2. **Do you see the light?** Siehst du das Licht?
3. **Are they coming tomorrow?** Kommen sie morgen?
4. **He is eating eggs.** Er isst Eier.
5. **She is drinking beer.** Sie trinkt Bier.
6. **I think about you every day.** Ich denke jeden Tag an dich.
7. **I am singing a song.** Ich singe ein Lied.
8. **Do you speak German?** Sprechen Sie Deutsch?
9. **I write many letters.** Ich schreibe viele Briefe.
10. **He is driving to Berlin.** Er fährt nach Berlin.

Day 22: To Do and To Make

In German there are two words for *to do*: *tun* and *machen*. What is the difference? *Machen* has a nuance of *to make*, but even still, people most often use *machen* to ask the question: *Was machen Sie?* (What are you doing?). *Tun* is more often used in set expressions, which you learned previously:

I'm sorry.	Es tut mir leid.	Lit. That does sorrow to me.
That hurts me.	Das tut mir weh.	Lit. That does pain to me.
That's good for me.	Das tut mir gut.	Lit. That does good to me.

Tun is most often used in these sentences, as well as other idiomatic expressions. If you ever feel like you don't know whether to use *tun* or *machen*, don't worry, a German speaker will understand no matter what you use.

Day 22 Vocabulary
1. **to do** tun |tat, getan|
2. **to answer** antworten *auf*
3. **to begin** beginnen |begann, begonnen|
4. **to receive / get** bekommen |bekam, bekommen|
5. **to stay / remain** bleiben |blieb, geblieben|
6. **to fly** fliegen |flog, geflogen|
7. **to cost** kosten
8. **to open** öffnen
9. **to close** schließen |schloss, geschlossen|
10. **to rain** regnen

Example Sentences
1. **What are you doing?** Was tust du?
2. **I am answering the question.** Ich antworte auf die Frage.
3. **When does it begin?** Wann beginnt es?
4. **Is she getting money?** Bekommt sie Geld?
5. **We are staying here.** Wir bleiben hier.
6. **I am flying to Paris.** Ich fliege nach Paris.
7. **How much does that cost?** Wie viel kostet das?
8. **When does it open?** Wann öffnet es?
9. **When does it close?** Wann schließt es?
10. **It is raining today.** Es regnet heute.

Day 23: Separable Prefixes

Some verbs in German have a separable prefix. An example of this is *aussehen* (to look). When you conjugate this verb, the prefix will move to the end of the sentence, Study the following example:

| **I look good.** | Ich sehe gut aus. |

Do you see how *aus* from *aussehen* moved to the end of the sentence? This can be confusing, because the last word of a sentence can change the meaning of the verb. As you start listening and speaking more, you are going to need to get used to holding all the information in your head until you hear the last word of the sentence, in order to understand its meaning. This is great practice for your short term memory!

Verbs with a separable prefix will be noted with an apostrophe. You will never write this apostrophe, it is simply to help you recognize verbs with a separable prefix.

Day 23 Vocabulary
1. **to look / appear** aus'sehen (sieht aus) |sah aus, ausgesehen|
2. **to stop** auf'hören
3. **to start / begin** an'fangen (fängt an) |fing an, angefangen|
4. **to listen** zu'hören
5. **to telephone / call** an'rufen |rief an, angerufen|
6. **to arrive** an'kommen |kam an, angekommen|
7. **to board / get *on*** ein'steigen *in* |stieg ein, eingestiegen|
8. **to watch TV** fern'sehen (sieht fern) |sah fern, ferngesehen|
9. **to take place** statt'finden |fand statt, stattgefunden|
10. **to suggest / propose** vor'schlagen (schlägt vor) |schlug vor, vorgeschlagen|

Example Sentences
1. **You look good.** Du siehst gut aus.
2. **She isn't stopping.** Sie hört nicht auf.
3. **When does it start?** Wann fängt es an?
4. **Are you listening?** Hörst du zu?
5. **I am calling Mr. Schmidt.** Ich rufe Herrn Schmidt an.
6. **When are we arriving?** Wann kommen wir an?
7. **I get on the train.** Ich steige in die Bahn ein.
8. **He is watching TV.** Er sieht fern.
9. **When does it take place?** Wann findet es statt?
10. **I am suggesting nothing.** Ich schlage nichts vor.

Day 24: Reflexive Verbs

Another class of verbs are called reflexive verbs. In the dictionary, reflexive verbs are preceded by *sich*. *Sich* can be translated as *myself / yourself / himself / herself / ourselves / themselves*. But most often, you don't actually translate the *sich* into English. *Sich* changes depending on the subject. Study the following table:

sich	
ich → mich	wir → uns
du → dich	ihr → euch
er → sich	sie → sich
sie → sich	Sie → sich
es → sich	

Notice for *er*, *sie*, *es*, *sie*, and *Sie*, there is no change. Though in the dictionary *sich* precedes the verb, when used it will follow the verb. Study the following examples with the verb *sich rasieren* (to shave):

I shave every day.	Ich rasiere mich jeden Tag.
Does he shave?	Rasiert er sich?

Again, the literal translation of the first sentence is: *I shave myself every day.* But most often, with reflexive verbs, you don't translate the *sich* into English.

<u>Day 24 Grammar Card</u>

sich	
mich	uns
dich	euch
sich	sich
sich	sich
sich	

<u>Day 24 Vocabulary</u>
1. **to shower** (sich) duschen
*Depending on the region, most speakers do not use *sich* with *duschen*, but some do.
2. **to hurry** sich beeilen
3. **to become angry *about*** sich ärgern *über*
4. **to remember *about*** sich erinnern *an* (Lit. remind oneself of)
5. **to sit down** sich setzen
6. **to get dressed** sich an'ziehen |zog an, angezogen|
7. **to move** sich bewegen
8. **to recover *from*** sich erholen *von*
9. **to shave** sich rasieren
10. **to consider** *dat.* sich überlegen
*_Sich überlegen_ is a special class of reflexive verb. It uses the dative case. This will covered in a later lesson.

<u>Example Sentences</u>
1. **I take a shower every day.** Ich dusche (mich) jeden Tag.
2. **She is hurrying.** Sie beeilt sich.
3. **That makes me very angry!** Das ärgert mich sehr!
4. **Do you remember that day?** Erinnerst du dich an jenen Tag?
5. **We are sitting ourselves on the floor.** Wir setzen uns auf den Boden.
6. **They are getting dressed.** Sie ziehen sich an.
7. **You all are moving quickly.** Ihr bewegt euch schnell.
8. **You are recovering well.** Sie erholen sich gut.
9. **He shaves every day.** Er rasiert sich jeden Tag.
10. **I am considering it.** Ich überlege mir es.

Another special class of verbs are called modal verbs. Modal verbs are definitely the most useful verbs in German, and English too! They are special because the *ich* conjugation is the same as *er / sie / es*. Study the following modal verbs and conjugation:

Modal Verbs	
want	wollen
shall	sollen
must / have to	müssen
may / be allowed to	dürfen
can	können
like	mögen

wollen (to want)			
ich	will	wir	wollen
du	willst	ihr	wollt
er	will	sie	wollen
sie	will	Sie	wollen
es	will		

Do you see how the *ich* and *er / sie / es* forms are the same? Also notice the *du* form uses the same stem with *-st* added. The other modal verbs all have irregular conjugations like this, and will be noted in the vocabulary section.

Modal verbs are always used with a main verb. When using modal verbs, the main verb will go to the end of the sentence. Study the following example:

I want to eat ice cream.	Ich will Eis essen.

Day 25 Grammar Card
1. **Modal verbs**
Same *ich / er / sie / es* forms.
Main verb to the end of the sentence.

Day 25 Vocabulary
1. **to want** wollen (will)
2. **shall / should** sollen (soll)
*English often uses the past tense *should* instead of *shall*. But in German, use the present tense.
3. **must / have to** müssen (muss) |musste, gemusst|
*A note about the negative form of this verb. In English, most sentences can use *must* or *have to* without a change in meaning. However, this is not true for *must not* and *don't have to*. In English, *must not* means that you are not allowed to do something. In German, *muss nicht* always means *doesn't have to*. If you want to say *must not,* as in, *not allowed to*, use *dürfen*.
4. **may / be allowed to** dürfen (darf) |durfte, gedurft|
5. **can** können (kann) |konnte, gekonnt|
6. **to like** mögen (mag) |mochte, gemocht|
7. **to mix / blend** mischen
8. **to tell** erzählen
9. **to run** laufen (läuft) |lief, gelaufen|
10. **to explain** erklären

Example Sentences
1. **I want to eat ice cream.** Ich will Eis essen.
2. **Shall we go?** Sollen wir gehen?
3. **She has to study every day.** Sie muss jeden Tag lernen.
4. **May I say something?** Darf ich etwas sagen?
5. **Can you speak slowly please?** Können Sie bitte langsam sprechen?
6. **Do you all like Pizza?** Mögt ihr Pizza?
7. **Can you mix that?** Kannst du das mischen?
8. **He is telling me a story.** Er erzählt mir eine Geschichte.
9. **We have to run quickly!** Wir müssen schnell laufen!
10. **Can you explain that?** Kannst du das erklären?

Day 26: Dative Verbs

Some verbs in German always use the dative case. Study the following example using *helfen* (to help):

| I am helping you. | Ich helfe dir. |

You may have originally thought the correct translation used the accusative: *Ich helfe dich.* But *helfen* always takes the dative case, so the correct translation is: *Ich helfe dir.* There are a number of verbs in German that use the dative case, and unfortunately, you just have to memorize them.

Reflexive verbs can also use the dative case. However, the dative form of *sich* is *sich.* So only the *ich* and *du* forms will change, using *mir* and *dir* instead of *mich* and *dich.* Study the following example using *sich vorstellen* (to imagine):

| I imagine. | Ich stelle mir vor. |

Reflexive verbs which can take an object are tricky, and use both accusative and dative. If the sentence has an object, *sich* becomes dative, without an object, *sich* is accusative. Study the following examples:

I am washing myself.	Ich wasche mich.
I am washing my hands.	Ich wasche mir die Hände.
I am getting dressed.	Ich ziehe mich an.
I am putting the shirt on.	Ich ziehe mir das Hemd an.

If a verb uses the dative case, it will be noted: *dat.*

Day 26 Vocabulary
1. **to help** *dat.* helfen (hilft) |half, geholfen|
2. **to imagine** *dat.* sich vor'stellen
3. **to forgive** *dat.* vergeben (vergibt) |vergab, vergeben|
4. **to follow** *dat.* folgen
5. **to belong to** *dat.* gehören
6. **to owe** *dat.* schulden
7. **to resemble** *dat.* ähneln
8. **to trust** *dat.* vertrauen
9. **to order / command** *dat.* befehlen (befiehlt) |befahl, befohlen|
10. **to contradict** *dat.* widersprechen (widerspricht) |widersprach, widersprochen|

Example Sentences
1. **Can you help me?** Kannst du mir helfen?
2. **Can you imagine that?** Kannst du dir das vorstellen?
3. **We can not forgive you.** Wir können dir nicht vergeben.
4. **Are you following me?** Folgen Sie mir?
5. **That belongs to him.** Das gehört ihm.
6. **You all owe her money.** Ihr schuldet ihr Geld.
7. **I resemble my mother.** Ich ähnele meiner Mutter.
8. **Can I trust you?** Kann ich dir vertrauen?
9. **He is ordering me to go.** Er befiehlt mir zu gehen.
10. **The child contradicts his parents.** Das Kind widerspricht seinen Eltern.

Day 27: Liking

Do you like German? Of course you do! Today's lesson covers liking things. Previously, you learned about the modal verb *mögen* (to like). When talking about liking a noun, Germans often use *mögen*, but when liking a verb, *gern* or *gerne* is added after the verb, depending on the region of the speaker. Study the following example:

I like ice cream.	Ich mag Eis.
I like to eat ice cream.	Ich esse gern Eis.

You can also use *gefallen* (to be pleasing) with the dative case.

I like ice cream.	Eis gefällt mir.	Lit. Ice cream pleases me.

To say something is your favorite, attach the prefix *Lieblings-* to the noun.

My favorite ice cream is chocolate.	Mein Lieblingseis ist Schokolade.

To ask people what kind of things they like, use the phrase *was für* (what kind of).

What kind of music do you like to listen to?	Was für Musik hören Sie gern?
What kind of ice cream do you like?	Was für Eis magst du?

Now you can ask people about their hobbies and what they like to do. To practice today, ask your friends: *Was machen Sie gern?*

<u>Day 27 Grammar Cards</u>
1. **to like (verb)**
(verb) + gern / gerne
2. **favorite (noun)**
Lieblings + (noun)

<u>Day 27 Vocabulary</u>
1. **ice / ice cream** das Eis
*This word is used for both ice (frozen water) and ice cream.
2. **to be pleasing** gefallen (gefällt) |gefiel, gefallen|
3. **favorite / darling** der Liebling (-e)
*This word can be used similarly to *sweetheart* or other names to call your significant other.
4. **what kind of** was für
5. **newspaper** die Zeitung (-en)
6. **magazine** die Zeitschrift (-en)
7. **government** die Regierung (-en)
8. **book** das Buch (ü, -er)
9. **page** die Seite (-n)
10. **room / space** der Raum (ä, -e)

<u>Example Sentences</u>
1. **I like to eat ice cream.** Ich esse gern Eis.
2. **You don't like that?** Gefällt dir das nicht?
3. **My favorite food is Pizza.** Mein Lieblingsessen ist Pizza.
4. **What kind of cars do you all like?** Was für Autos gefallen euch?
5. **Does he like to read the newspaper?** Liest er gern die Zeitung?
6. **What is her favorite magazine?** Was ist ihre Lieblingszeitschrift?
7. **I don't like the government.** Die Regierung gefällt mir nicht.
8. **She is giving him her favorite book.** Sie gibt ihm ihr Lieblingsbuch.
9. **They are sending me several pages.** Sie schicken mir mehrere Seiten.
10. **How do they like the room?** Wie gefällt ihnen der Raum?

Day 28: Imperative Form, Commands

German has three different imperative forms depending on the subject: *du*, *ihr*, and *Sie*. The *Sie* form simply switches the position of the subject and verb, just like a question. Unlike English, *you* (*Sie*) is not dropped. Study the following examples:

Please sign here.	Unterschreiben Sie bitte hier.
Please take out a piece of paper.	Nehmen Sie bitte ein Blatt Papier heraus.

To make *ihr* commands, drop *-en* and add *-t* to the verb stem, just like the present tense conjugation.

Give me the money!	Gebt mir das Geld!
Eat until you all are full.	Esst bis ihr satt seid.

To make *du* commands with weak verbs, drop *-en* and use the unconjugated stem.

Stop that!	Hör damit auf!
Do it quickly!	Mach schnell!

Strong verbs that have a vowel change keep the vowel change in *du* commands. But verbs that add an umlaut in the present tense don't add one in the imperative form.

Eat your dinner!	Iss dein Abendessen!
Drive faster!	Fahr schneller!

Some verbs also add an *-e* for *du* commands. This is because the pronunciation of these verbs would sound strange without the vowel.

Work faster!	Arbeite schneller!
Breathe in deeper!	Atme tiefer ein!

Two verbs have a special *du* command: *wissen* (wisse) and *werden* (werde). *Sein* is irregular:

sein (imperative)	
du	sei
ihr	seid
Sie	seien

Day 28 Grammar Cards

1. **Commands (Sie)**
Switch subject and verb.
2. **Commands (ihr)**
Drop -*en* add -*t*.
3. **Commands (du)**
(weak) Drop -*en*.
(strong) Drop -*en*, drop umlaut, keep vowel change.
wissen (wisse)
werden (werde)
4.

sein (imperative)	
du	sei
ihr	seid
Sie	seien

Day 28 Vocabulary

1. **already** schon
2. **way / path / road** der Weg (-e)
*In addition to physical roads and paths, *der Weg* can also be used as *the way to do something*, or *the method*.
3. **same / identical** gleich
4. **alone** allein
5. **type / kind / sort** die Art (-en)
*Don't use *die Art* to ask *What kind of*. Use *was für*.
6. **a little bit / a small amount** ein bisschen
7. **quiet / calm** ruhig
8. **little / few / less** wenig
9. **truth** die Wahrheit (-en)
10. **important** wichtig

Example Sentences

1. **Do it already!** Mach schon!
2. **Drive on this path.** Fahren Sie auf diesem Weg.
3. **Drink the same drink. (You all)** Trinkt das gleiche Getränk.
4. **Leave me alone!** Lass mich allein!
5. **Cook me this type of dish.** Koch mir diese Art von Gericht.
6. **Give me a little bit.** Gib mir ein bisschen.
7. **Be quiet.** Sei ruhig.
8. **Eat less candies.** Iss weniger Süßigkeiten.
9. **Tell me the truth.** Erzähl mir die Wahrheit.
10. **Write down the important things.** Schreiben Sie bitte die wichtigen Sachen auf.

Day 29: Future Tense

The future tense is quite easy in German. Like English, you can simply use the present tense with a time word to indicate that you are talking about the future:

| I'm going to Berlin tomorrow. | Ich fahre morgen nach Berlin. |

English uses the verb *will*. German uses *werden* (to become), which has a slightly irregular conjugation. Like modal verbs, using *werden* will cause the main verb to move to the end of the sentence. Study the following conjugation and example:

werden (to become)			
ich	werde	wir	werden
du	wirst	ihr	werdet
er	wird	sie	werden
sie	wird	Sie	werden
es	wird		

| I will go to Berlin tomorrow. | Ich werde morgen nach Berlin fahren. |

Day 29 Grammar Card
1. **Future tense**
(werden) + end of sentence (infinitive)

Day 29 Vocabulary
1. **to become** werden (du wirst, es wird) |wurde, geworden|
2. **to build** bauen
3. **to permit / allow** erlauben
4. **to put / place / set (vertical / standing)** stellen
*This is the default word for *put / place.*
5. **to set / place / put (sitting)** setzen
*Note the reflexive form of this verb you have already learned, *sich sestzen* (to sit down).
6. **to put / stick / plug in** stecken
7. **to destroy** zerstören
8. **to inquire *about*** sich erkundigen *nach*
9. **to rescue *from*** retten *vor / aus*
Retten vor and *retten aus* both mean *to rescue from. Retten vor* is used when you rescue something from a person or an intangible bad situation. *Retten aus* is used when you rescue someone from a tangible situation, like a burning building or car.
10. **to collapse** ein'stürzen

Example Sentences
1. **The weather is becoming better.** Das Wetter wird besser.
2. **We will build a city.** Wir werden eine Stadt bauen.
3. **Will you allow it?** Wirst du das erlauben?
4. **I am putting it on the internet.** Ich stelle es ins Internet.
5. **I will put the baby on the chair.** Ich werde das Baby auf den Stuhl setzen.
6. **Will he plug it into the outlet?** Wird er es in die Steckdose stecken?
7. **She will destroy everything!** Sie wird alles zerstören!
8. **I am inquiring about the news.** Ich erkundige mich nach den Nachrichten.
9. **Will you rescue me from him?** Wirst du mich vor ihm retten?
10. **The building will collapse!** Das Gebäude wird einstürzen!

Day 30: Present Perfect Tense

There are two main forms of past tense in German, just like English, called Präteritum / Imperfekt (preterite / simple past) and Perfekt (present perfect). Unlike English, German uses the simple past for writing, and the present perfect for speaking. There are a few exceptions, if you are telling a long story, it's okay to switch to the simple past.

To make the present perfect tense, English uses *have* + past participle. German uses *sein* or *haben* + past participle. Use *sein* when the verb shows motion, movement, or a change in state. Verbs like *gehen*, *sterben*, and *sein,* will use *sein* instead of *haben*. Like modal verbs and the future tense, using *sein* or *haben* will send the main verb to the end of the sentence. Study the following examples:

| **I ate eggs.** | Ich habe Eier gegessen. |
| **I went to Hamburg.** | Ich bin nach Hamburg gefahren. |

Like the present tense, the past tense in German has multiple English meanings. The first example sentence could be translated as: *I ate eggs, I have eaten eggs, I have been eating eggs,* or *I did eat eggs*

To conjugate the past participle, add the prefix *ge-*. Verbs starting with a vowel add *geg-*. If a verb has a separable prefix, *ge-* goes in the middle. If a verb starts with *be- pro- ver- zer-* or ends with *-ieren*, don't add *ge-*. If you have trouble remembering this, another way to remember it, is that verbs with stress on the second syllable don't add *ge-*. Some strong verbs also have a vowel change. Weak verbs will drop *-en* and add *-t*. Weak verbs that end in *-ten* will drop *-en* and add *-et*. This is a lot of information, so study the following examples:

Infinitive → Participle Add *ge-*, weak verbs drop *-en* add *-t*	
gehen → gegangen (vowel change)	fragen → gefragt
essen → gegessen (*geg-*)	antworten → geantwortet (add *-et*)
anrufen → angerufen (separable prefix)	zerstören → zerstört (no *ge-*)

When *sein* and *haben* were first introduced in this book, the participles were not included. Sein is irregular, the participle is *gewesen*. The participle of *haben* is formed like a weak verb, *gehabt.*

Day 30 Grammar Cards
1. Present perfect tense
Used for speaking. Four meanings.
(sein / haben) + (past participle)
Don't add *ge-* to verbs with *be- pro- ver- zer- -ieren.*
gewesen (sein)
gehabt (haben)
2. Past participle (strong)
Possible vowel change, add *ge-*.
3. Past participle (weak)
Drop *-en*, add *ge-, -t.*

<u>Day 30 Vocabulary</u>
1. **to dream *about*** träumen *von*
2. **to tidy up** auf'räumen
3. **to clean / wipe / polish** putzen
4. **to clean** sauber'machen
5. **to clean / purify** reinigen
*The adjective *sauber* means *clean*. The adjective *rein* means *pure*.
6. **to ride** reiten |ritt, geritten|
7. **to press / push** drücken
Drücken is used when you press things like buttons.
8. **to push / kick** stoßen (stößt) |stieß, gestoßen|
Stoßen has a feeling of disturbing or causing harm.
9. **to push** schieben |schob, geschoben|
Schieben is used in all normal, non-violent forms of pushing.
10. **to hide *from*** verstecken *vor*

<u>Example Sentences</u>
1. **Did you dream about me?** Hast du von mir geträumt?
2. **They tidied up the room.** Sie haben das Zimmer aufgeräumt.
3. **She cleaned the counter.** Sie hat die Theke geputzt.
4. **He cleaned the floor.** Er hat den Boden saubergemacht.
5. **We purified the water.** Wir haben das Wasser gereinigt.
6. **I rode the horse.** Ich bin auf dem Pferd geritten.
7. **Did you press the button?** Haben Sie den Knopf gedrückt?
8. **The child pushed the little girl.** Das Kind hat das Mädchen gestoßen.
9. **I pushed the car.** Ich habe das Auto geschoben.
10. **I hid the present from my mother.** Ich habe das Geschenk vor meiner Mutter versteckt.

Day 31: Future Past Tense

Is this an X-men movie? This grammar is used to talk about what will have been done in the future. The construction is almost the exact same as English. Use the verb *werden* + the past participle and auxiliary verb. Since *werden* is now occupying the spot after the subject, not only the participle, but also the unconjugated auxiliary verb will go the end of the sentence. Study the following examples:

Tomorrow I will have written my essay.	Morgen werde ich meinen Aufsatz geschrieben haben.
Next month he will have already gone back to Germany.	Nächsten Monat wird er schon nach Deutschland zurückgefahren sein.

Day 31 Grammar Card
1. **Future past tense**
(werden) + (past participle) + (sein / haben)

Day 31 Vocabulary
1. **to end / come to a close** ab'schließen |schloss ab, abgeschlossen|
2. **to end (intransitive)** enden
3. **to end (transitive)** beenden
*Transitive means the verb can take an object. *Enden* cannot take an object.
4. **to be concerned with / occupy oneself** *with* sich befassen *mit*
5. **to be busy / occupy oneself** *with* sich beschäftigen *mit*
*Important derivatives: *beschäftig* (busy) and B*eschäftigung* (occupation).
6. **to observe** beobachten
*Careful with the pronunciation. *Beo* is not pronounced *beyo,* but rather *beh oh.*
7. **to walk** spazieren
Spazieren is often paired with *gehen*, as in, *to go walking. Ich gehe spazieren.*
8. **to fulfill** erfüllen
9. **to carry out / execute** aus'führen
10. **to be adequate** genügen
*The adjective *genug* means *enough* or *sufficient.*

Example Sentences
1. **The trial will have come to a close.** Das Gerichtsverfahren wird abgeschlossen sein.
2. **The film will have ended.** Der Film wird geendet haben.
3. **I will have ended the relationship.** Ich werde die Beziehung beendet haben.
4. **He will have concerned himself with something.** Er wird sich mit etwas befasst haben.
5. **She will have occupied herself with something.** Sie wird sich mit etwas beschäftigt haben.
6. **We will have observed it.** Wir werden es beobachtet haben.
7. **They will have walked through the park.** Sie werden durch den Park spaziert sein.
8. **I will have fulfilled the requirements.** Ich werde die Anforderungen erfüllt haben.
9. **He will have carried out the order.** Er wird den Auftrag ausgeführt haben.
10. **It will have been adequate.** Es wird genügt haben.

Day 32: Simple Past, Preterite Tense

Today's lesson covers the simple past (Präteritum / Imperfekt). The simple past is used in writing, or when you are telling a long story, and also with certain verbs. *Sein, haben,* and modal verbs use the simple past even in speaking. Like modal verbs, the *ich* conjugation is the same as the *er / sie / es* conjugation. For the other pronouns, also add the normal conjugation for the pronoun.

Like English, strong verbs are irregular in the simple past tense, and will have a vowel change. Once you become more familiar with the strong verbs, you should be able to guess what the vowel change will be, because verbs with the same main vowel have similar vowel changes, just like in English. Study the following conjugations:

sein (to be)			
ich	war	wir	waren
du	warst	ihr	wart
er	war	sie	waren
sie	war	Sie	waren
es	war		

haben (to have)			
ich	hatte	wir	hatten
du	hattest	ihr	hattet
er	hatte	sie	hatten
sie	hatte	Sie	hatten
es	hatte		

tragen (to carry)			
ich	trug	wir	trugen
du	trugst	ihr	trugt
er	trug	sie	trugen
sie	trug	Sie	trugen
es	trug		

All weak verbs follow the same conjugation. Drop -en and add -te.

legen (to lay)			
ich	legte	wir	legten
du	legtest	ihr	legten
er	legte	sie	legten
sie	legte	Sie	legten
es	legte		

Day 32 Grammar Card

1. **Simple past**
Used in writing, telling long stories.
Used often with *sein*, *haben*, and modal verbs.
Same *ich / er / sie / es* conjugation.
(weak) Drop -en add -te.

Day 32 Vocabulary

1. **to comprehend / grasp** begreifen |begriff, begriffen|
2. **to bend** biegen |bog, gebogen|
3. **to break** brechen (bricht) |brach, gebrochen|
4. **to freeze** frieren |fror, gefroren|
5. **to pour** ein'gießen |goss ein, eingegossen|
6. **to lend** leihen |lieh, geliehen|
7. **to rip** zerreißen |zerriss, zerrissen|
8. **to scream** schreien |schrie, geschrien|
9. **to stay quiet / be still** schweigen |schwieg, geschwiegen|
10. **to hit** schlagen (schlägt) |schlug, geschlagen|

Example Sentences

1. **We grasped the concept.** Wir begriffen das Konzept.
2. **They bent the pole.** Sie bogen den Mast.
3. **You broke my heart.** Du brachst mein Herz.
4. **I went outside and froze.** Ich ging nach draußen und fror.
5. **He poured the wine.** Er goss den Wein ein.
6. **She lent him the money.** Sie lieh ihm das Geld.
7. **He ripped his pants.** Er zerriss seine Hose.
8. **The baby screamed loudly.** Das Baby schrie laut.
9. **She screamed, and he remained quiet.** Sie schrie und er schwieg.
10. **They hit me.** Sie schlugen mich.

Day 33: Past Perfect Tense

Today's lesson covers *Plusquamperfekt*. Say it out loud, *Plus-quam-perfekt*. It's such a fun word to say! The past perfect tense is used to talk about two events in the past. One event will happen before the other, but both are in the past. The grammar construction is the same as the present perfect, but using the past tense of the auxiliary verb. Don't forget, verbs that show motion or a change in state will use *sein* instead of *haben*:

| I had eaten a cake. | Ich hatte eine Kuchen gegessen. |
| I had become fat. | Ich war dick geworden. |

Of course, this grammar is used to talk about two events in the past. Combining clauses will be covered later in the book. But basically, the auxiliary verb in the relative clause will go to the end. Study the following examples:

| I went to the gym, because I had become fat. | Ich bin ins Fitnessstudio gegangen, weil ich dick geworden war. |
| I had eaten a cake before I ate dinner. | Ich hatte einen Kuchen gegessen, bevor ich Abendessen gegessen habe. |

Notice the auxiliary verb goes to the end of the second clause. If you rearrange the clause order, and put the main clause second, the subject and verb of the main clause will switch places, and the verbs will directly follow each other. Study the following examples:

| Because I had become fat, I went to the gym. | Weil ich dick geworden war, bin ich ins Fitnessstudio gegangen. |
| Before I ate dinner, I had eaten a cake. | Bevor ich Abendessen gegessen habe, hatte ich einen Kuchen gegessen. |

This is the most common construction. When using the *Plusquamperfekt*, the main clause is usually second, like in the above example, and the verbs will directly follow each other.

People often use the simple past with *Plusquamperfekt*, because you are often explaining a longer story. Study the following example using the simple past and present perfect:

| After I had studied German, I studied Japanese. | Nachdem ich Deutsch gelernt hatte, lernte ich Japanisch. |
| After I had studied German, I studied Japanese. | Nachdem ich Deutsch gelernt hatte, habe ich Japanisch gelernt. |

To practice this grammar, talk about what you did yesterday, use two events and say when they happened. If there is no one to listen to your story, just talk to the mirror!

Day 33 Grammar Card
1. **Plusquamperfekt**
[main clause] past participle of (sein / haben) + (past participle)
[relative clause] (sein / haben) + (past participle)
If relative clause come first, verbs directly follow each other.

Day 33 Vocabulary
1. **store** der Laden (ä)
2. **church** die Kirche (n)
3. **monument / memorial** das Denkmal (ä, -er)
4. **building** das Gebäude
5. **library** die Bibliothek (-en)
6. **hospital** das Krankenhaus (ä, -er)
7. **movie theater** das Kino (-s)
8. **pharmacy** die Apotheke (-n)
9. **factory** die Fabrik (-en)
10. **butcher shop** die Metzgerei (-en)

Example Sentences
1. **I had gone to the store before I came home.**
Ich war zum Laden gegangen, bevor ich nach Hause kam.
2. **I had prayed before I went to church.**
Ich hatte gebetet, bevor ich in die Kirche ging.
3. **After I had gone to the memorial, I bought a souvenir.**
Nachdem ich zum Denkmal gegangen war, kaufte ich ein Souvenir.
4. **He had bought the building, before he became a millionaire.**
Er hatte das Gebäude gekauft, bevor er ein Millionär geworden ist.
5. **After I had read the book, I went back to the library.**
Nachdem ich das Buch gelesen hatte, ging ich zur Bibliothek zurück.
6. **After she had gone to the hospital, she became sick.**
Nachdem sie ins Krankenhaus gegangen war, wurde sie krank.
7. **I had gone to the bank before I went to the movie theater.**
Ich war zur Bank gegangen, bevor ich ins Kino ging.
8. **After I had gone to the pharmacy, I bought medicine.**
Nachdem ich zur Apotheke gegangen war, kaufte ich Medizin.
9. **They had torn down the factory, before they built the new building.**
Sie hatten die Fabrik abgerissen, bevor sie das neue Gebäude gebaut haben.
10. **I had already bought meat before you went to the butcher shop.**
Ich hatte schon Fleisch gekauft, bevor du zur Metzgerei gegangen bist.

Day 34: Verbs as Nouns

You may have noticed already that the majority of the vocabulary thus far has been verbs. That's because almost every verb can also be converted into a noun. Like in English, many nouns in German are derived from their verb counterparts. Some verbs can simply be used in their infinitive forms as nouns, some use the past tense with a vowel change. Study the following examples:

The food.	Das Essen.
The speech.	Das Sprechen.
The drink.	Das Getränk.
The conversation.	Das Gespräch.

Like in English, adding -er or -erin to many verb stems will denote a person who does that verb:

The speaker.	Der Sprecher.
The baker.	Die Bäckerin.

Another common construction is to replace -en with -ung:

to govern	regieren
The government.	Die Regierung.
to introduce	einleiten
The introduction.	Die Einleitung.

Go back and look at the verbs you have learned thus far and try to guess what their noun counterparts would be. I'll bet you can guess most of them correctly!

Day 34 Vocabulary
1. **corporation** das Unternehmen
2. **government** die Regierung (-en)
3. **development / trend / evolution** die Entwicklung (-en)
4. **decision** die Entscheidung (-en)
5. **sacrifice / victim** das Opfer
6. **report / record** der Bericht (-e)
7. **pressure** der Druck (ü, -e)
8. **war** der Krieg (-e)
9. **pronunciation** die Aussprache (-n)
10. **grave** das Grab (ä, -er)

Example Sentences
1. **The corporation paid taxes.** Das Unternehmen bezahlte Steuern.
2. **The government passes laws.** Die Regierung verabschiedet Gesetze.
3. **No one expected this development.** Diese Entwicklung hat niemand erwartet.
4. **The decision was terrible.** Die Entscheidung war furchtbar.
5. **The accident caused many victims.** Der Umfall forderte viele Opfer.
6. **Give me the report.** Gib mir den Bericht.
7. **I can't take the pressure.** Ich kann den Druck nicht ertragen.
8. **When will the war end?** Wann wird der Krieg enden?
9. **The pronunciation of this word is hard.** Die Aussprache dieses Wortes ist schwer.
10. **I visit her grave every year.** Ich besuche ihr Grab jedes Jahr.

Day 35: Verb Practice

Now that you've learned all the basics of verbs, spend the next week reviewing and practicing all of the grammar and new vocabulary.

<u>Day 35 Vocabulary</u>
1. **to name** nennen |nannte, genannt|
2. **to show** zeigen
3. **to lead** führen
4. **to bring** bringen |brachte, gebracht|
5. **to live** leben
6. **to be valid** gelten (gilt) |galt, gegolten|
7. **to win** gewinnen |gewann, gewonnen|
8. **to need** brauchen
9. **to discuss / debate** diskutieren
10. **to study (subject / major)** studieren

<u>Example Sentences</u>
1. **I am naming her Anja.** Ich nenne sie Anja.
2. **They are showing it now.** Sie zeigen es jetzt.
3. **He is leading the tour.** Er führt die Tour.
4. **The postman is bringing a letter.** Der Briefträger bringt einen Brief.
5. **It's alive!** Es lebt!
6. **The Passport is valid until next year.** Der Reisepass gilt bis nächstes Jahr.
7. **You all will win!** Ihr werdet gewinnen!
8. **Do you need that?** Brauchen Sie das?
9. **What are you discussing?** Was diskutieren Sie?
10. **We study math at MIT.** Wir studieren Mathematik am MIT.

Day 36: Verb Practice

Day 36 Vocabulary
1. **to try / attempt** versuchen
2. **to wear / carry** tragen (trägt) |trug, getragen|
3. **to sit / be sitting** sitzen |saß, gesessen|
4. **to pull / move** ziehen |zog, gezogen|
5. **to shine / appear / seem** scheinen |schien, geschienen|
6. **to fall** fallen (fällt) |fiel, gefallen|
7. **to get / keep / preserve** erhalten (erhält) |erhielt, erhalten|
Erhalten has many possible translations. The core meaning is *to completely hold / stop*. This core meaning can help to derive the other possible translations: *to get, to keep, to preserve, to save, to sustain, to gain, to maintain, to support, to remain.*
8. **to meet** sich treffen (trifft) |traf, getroffen|
9. **to reach / achieve** erreichen
10. **to originate / come *from*** entstehen *aus* |entstand, entstanden|

Example Sentences
1. **What are they trying?** Was versuchen sie?
2. **I am carrying you.** Ich trage dich.
3. **They are sitting on the floor.** Sie sitzen auf dem Boden.
4. **He is pulling the suitcase.** Er zieht den Koffer.
5. **That seems to be good.** Das scheint gut zu sein.
6. **She is falling quickly.** Sie fällt schnell.
7. **The banks are getting subsidies.** Die Banken erhalten Subventionen.
8. **I am meeting my friend.** Ich treffe mich mit meinem Freund.
9. **Are you achieving the goal?** Erreichst du das Ziel?
10. **Flowers come from seeds.** Blumen entstehen aus Samen.

Day 37: Verb Practice

Day 37 Vocabulary
1. **to mean** bedeuten
2. **to search / look** *for* suchen *nach*
3. **to give** geben (gibt) |gab, gegeben|
4. **to read** lesen (liest) |las, gelesen|
5. **to take** nehmen (nimmt) |nahm, genommen|
6. **to travel** reisen
7. **to sleep** schlafen (schläft) |schlief, geschlafen|
8. **to stand** stehen |stand, gestanden|
9. **to understand** verstehen |verstand, verstanden|
10. **to live / reside** wohnen

Example Sentences
1. **What does this word mean?** Was bedeutet dieses Wort?
2. **Are you looking for me?** Suchst du nach mir?
3. **I give him food every year.** Ich gebe ihm jedes Jahr Essen.
4. **We read books every day.** Wir lesen jeden Tag Bücher.
5. **He is taking the money.** Er nimmt das Geld.
6. **She is traveling to Germany.** Sie reist nach Deutschland.
7. **I don't sleep enough.** Ich schlafe nicht genug.
8. **They are standing by the wall.** Sie stehen an der Wand.
9. **Do you understand that?** Verstehst du das?
10. **Where do you live?** Wo wohnen Sie?

Day 38: Verb Practice

Day 38 Vocabulary
1. **to excuse** entschuldigen
2. **to know (information)** wissen (weiß) |wusste, gewusst|
3. **to know (people)** kennen |kannte, gekannt|
4. **to be lacking / missing** fehlen
*As a noun: *der Fehler* (mistake)
5. **to find** finden |fand, gefunden|
6. **to lie (position)** liegen |lag, gelegen|
7. **to lay / lay down** legen
*Don't forget, *lie* is intransitive (no object) and *lay* is transitive (takes an object).
8. **to be called (name)** heißen |hieß, geheißen|
9. **to believe *in*** glauben *an*
10. **to hold / halt / stop (moving)** halten (hält) |hielt, gehalten|
*You previously learned *aufhören* (to stop). *Aufhören* means to stop doing something. *Halten* means to stop moving, just like *to halt* in English. *Halten* can also mean to hold something in your hands.

Example Sentences
1. **I will excuse the absence.** Ich werde die Abwesenheit entschuldigen.
2. **I don't know the answer.** Ich weiß die Antwort nicht.
3. **Do you know her?** Kennst du sie?
4. **Something is missing still.** Etwas fehlt noch.
5. **She finds the money.** Sie findet das Geld.
6. **He is lying on the bed.** Er liegt auf dem Bett.
7. **He is laying it on the table.** Er legt es auf den Tisch.
8. **I'm called Jack.** Ich heiße Jack.
9. **They don't believe in God.** Sie glauben nicht an Gott.
10. **The bus is stopping.** Der Bus hält.

Day 39: Verb Practice

Day 39 Vocabulary
1. **to watch** *dat.* zu'sehen (sieht zu) |sah zu, zugesehen|
2. **to miss (train / bus)** verpassen
3. **to miss (person)** vermissen
4. **to pass / go by (time)** vergehen |verging, vergangen|
5. **to move / change residence** umziehen |zog um, umgezogen|
6. **to change clothes** sich umziehen |zog um, umgezogen|
7. **to happen / occur** geschehen (geschieht) |geschah, geschehen|
8. **to happen / occur** passieren
Geschehen and *passieren* are basically interchangeable, but there are some subtle differences. *Passieren* has a nuance similar to *It came to pass that...* and is more often used when things happen to you. *Geschehen* usually refers to events. English uses the proposition *to,* German uses *mit.* However, pronouns don't require *mit.* For example: **What happened to the food?** *Was ist mit dem Essen passiert?* **What happened to you?** *Was ist dir passiert?* There are also a some idiomatic phrases: **No matter what happens...** *Egal, was passiert...* **There's no use crying over spilled milk.** *Was geschehen ist, ist geschehen.*
9. **to appear** erscheinen |erschien, erschienen|
10. **to recognize** erkennen

Example Sentences
1. **I watch the ducks every day.** Ich sehe den Enten jeden Tag zu.
2. **I miss the bus every day.** Ich verpasse den Bus jeden Tag.
3. **She misses him.** Sie vermisst ihn.
4. **Time goes by so quickly.** Die Zeit vergeht so schnell.
5. **They are moving to Germany.** Sie ziehen nach Deutschland um.
6. **I have to change.** Ich muss mich umziehen.
7. **It happens every day.** Das geschieht jeden Tag.
8. **Nothing is happening.** Nichts passiert.
9. **He shall appear soon.** Er soll bald erscheinen.
10. **Do you recognize that man?** Erkennst du den Mann?

Day 40: Verb Practice

<u>Day 40 Vocabulary</u>
1. **to pick up** auf'heben |hob auf, aufgehoben|
2. **to turn on** an'machen
*This can be used like in English to say that you are attracted to someone.
3. **to turn off** aus'machen
Ausmachen has many possible translations. The literal translation *to make out* can help to derive the other translations: *to be able to see, to bother someone, to make a difference, to be about, to add up to, to agree.*
4. **to open** auf'machen
*You've already learned *öffnen* (to open), *aufmachen* is more casual.
5. **to close** zu'machen
*You've already learned *schließen* (to close), *zumachen* is more casual.
6. **to invite** ein'laden (lädt ein) |lud ein, eingeladen|
7. **to wake up** auf'wachen
8. **to tie** zusammen'binden (bindet) |band zusammen, zusammengebunden|
9. **to sound** klingen |klang, geklungen|
10. **to be right / vote** stimmen
Stimmen is most often used to say that something is correct. If used with a pronoun, it means *to vote*.

<u>Example Sentences</u>
1. **I am picking up the pieces.** Ich hebe die Stücke auf.
2. **He is turning the light on.** Er macht das Licht an.
3. **She is turning the light off.** Sie macht das Licht aus.
4. **They are opening the door.** Sie machen die Tür auf.
5. **We are closing the door.** Wir machen die Tür zu.
6. **I am inviting you all.** Ich lade euch ein.
7. **You always wake up early.** Du wachst immer früh auf.
8. **Could you tie this please?** Könnten Sie das bitte zusammenbinden?
9. **This music sounds good.** Diese Musik klingt gut.
10. **Is that right?** Stimmt das?

Day 41: Verb Practice

Day 41 Vocabulary
1. **to touch** an'fassen
Anfassen has the nuance of touching something with intent.
2. **to touch / come into contact** berühren
Berühren has the nuance of touching something on accident or without intention.
3. **to surprise** überraschen
4. **to marry** heiraten
5. **to complain about** sich beschweren *über*
6. **to worry about** sich sorgen *um*
7. **to doubt** bezweifeln
8. **to experience** erleben
9. **to shape / form** gestalten
10. **to kiss** küssen

Example Sentences
1. **He touched my arm.** Er fasste meinen Arm an.
2. **She touched my skin.** Sie berührte meine Haut.
3. **The toy surprised me.** Das Spielzeug überraschte mich.
4. **We will never marry.** Wir werden nie heiraten.
5. **He always complains about the food.** Er beschwert sich immer über das Essen.
6. **They are worrying about you.** Sie sorgen sich um dich.
7. **I doubt that you have money.** Ich bezweifele, dass du Geld hast.
8. **I have experienced many things.** Ich habe viele Sachen erlebt.
9. **He shapes his own life.** Er gestaltet sein eigenes Leben.
10. **She won't kiss me.** Sie küsst mich nicht.

Day 42: Verb Practice

<u>Day 42 Vocabulary</u>
1. **to offer** an'bieten |bot an, angeboten|
2. **to ask / beg** *for* bitten *um* |bat, gebeten|
3. **to catch / capture** fangen (fängt) |fing, gefangen|
4. **to lie / fib** lügen |log, gelogen|
5. **to shoot** schiessen |schoss, geschossen|
6. **to cut / carve** schneiden |schnitt, geschnitten|
7. **to jump** springen |sprang, gesprungen|
8. **to steal** stehlen (stiehlt) |stahl, gestohlen|
9. **to rob** aus'rauben
10. **to kill** töten

<u>Example Sentences</u>
1. **They offered a discount.** Sie boten eine Ermäßigung an.
2. **She begged for forgiveness.** Sie bat um Vergebung.
3. **We captured the criminal.** Wir fingen den Verbrecher.
4. **He lies when he opens his mouth.** Er lügt wenn er den Mund aufmacht.
5. **The soldier shot into the air.** Der Soldat schoss in die Luft.
6. **I cut the meat into pieces.** Ich schnitt das Fleisch in Stücke.
7. **You jumped very high.** Du sprangst sehr hoch.
8. **He stole a watch.** Er stahl eine Uhr.
9. **They robbed the store.** Sie raubten den Laden aus.
10. **You all killed the soldiers.** Ihr tötetet die Soldaten.

Day 43: Verb Practice

Day 43 Vocabulary

1. **to exist** bestehen |bestand, bestanden|
Bestehen can also be translated as: *to be made of / to consist of.* In which case it will take the preposition *aus*.
2. **to bleed** bluten
3. **to distort / disfigure** entstellen
4. **to scare / frighten** erschrecken
5. **to reveal / uncover** auf'decken
6. **to disappear** verschwinden |verschwand, verschwunden|
7. **to assume / suppose** vermuten
8. **to cheat / defraud** betrügen |betrog, betrogen|
9. **to fit / match / suit** passen
10. **to contribute** *to* bei'tragen *zu* (trägt bei) |trug bei, beigetragen|

Example Sentences

1. **The company has existed since 2001.** Die Firma besteht seit 2001.
2. **My finger is bleeding.** Mein Finger blutet.
3. **Your face is distorted.** Dein Gesicht ist entstellt.
4. **His face frightened the children.** Sein Gesicht hat die Kinder erschreckt.
5. **The truth will be revealed.** Die Wahrheit wird aufgedeckt werden.
6. **She disappeared quickly.** Sie verschwand schnell.
7. **That can not be assumed.** Das kann nicht vermutet werden.
8. **We defrauded the company.** Wir betrogen die Firma.
9. **The tie suits you.** Die Krawatte passt zu dir.
10. **Will you contribute to our venture?** Wirst du zu unserem Projekt beitragen?

Day 44: Accusative Prepositions

German prepositions always take a certain case. Study the following prepositions which always take the accusative case:

Accusative Prepositions	
until	bis
through	durch
for	für
without	ohne
against	gegen
around	um

When using these prepositions, the nouns will always be accusative. Study the following examples:

I am waiting until tomorrow.	Ich warte bis morgen.
I am walking through the forest.	Ich spaziere durch den Wald.
That is for me.	Das ist für mich.
We are going without you.	Wir gehen ohne dich.
He is fighting against the enemy.	Er kämpft gegen den Feind.
She runs around the sea.	Sie rennt um den See.

Accusative prepositions will be noted *akk.* to remind you that they always use the accusative case.

Day 44 Vocabulary
1. **through** *akk.* durch
2. **for** *akk.* für
3. **without** *akk.* ohne
4. **against** *akk.* gegen
5. **around** *akk.* um
6. **until** *akk.* bis
7. **to wait *for*** warten *auf*
8. **to create** erschaffen
9. **to lose** verlieren |verlor, verloren|
10. **to portray / depict** dar'stellen

Example Sentences
1. **I am walking through the forest.** Ich spaziere durch den Wald.
2. **That is for me.** Das ist für mich.
3. **We are going without you.** Wir gehen ohne dich.
4. **He is fighting against the enemy.** Er kämpft gegen den Feind.
5. **She runs around the sea.** Sie rennt um den See.
6. **We are watching TV until tomorrow.** Wir sehen bis morgen fern.
7. **They are waiting for you.** Sie warten auf dich.
8. **I am creating a monster!** Ich erschaffe ein Monster!
9. **She is losing her mind without him.** Ohne ihn verliert sie ihren Verstand.
10. **The picture portrays an animal.** Das Bild stellt ein Tier dar.

Day 45: Dative Prepositions

The following prepositions always take the dative case:

Dative Prepositions	
out / from	aus
outside of / except for	außer
by / with	bei
with	mit
after	nach
since	sei
from / of	von
to	zu
according to	gemäß
across from	gegenüber

You may notice some prepositions have multiple meanings. Mastering prepositions in German will take some trial and error. Consider the sentences: *She is angry with me. She is angry at me.* Which is correct? Is it *with* or *at*? What is the actual meaning of *with* and *at*? Does anyone really know? The same problem happens in German. In many cases, more than one preposition can fit, and the prepositions themselves have many translations based on what verb they follow.

Dative prepositions will be noted *dat.* to remind you that they always use the dative case.

Day 45 Vocabulary
1. **out / from** *dat.* aus
2. **outside of / except for** *dat.* außer
3. **by / with / at** *dat.* bei
4. **with** *dat.* mit
5. **after** *dat.* nach
6. **since** *dat.* seit
7. **from / of** *dat.* von
8. **to** *dat.* zu
9 **according to** *dat.* gemäß
10. **across from** *dat.* gegenüber

Example Sentences
1. **He is coming out of the house.** Er kommt aus dem Haus.
2. **Except for me, she likes everyone.** Außer mir mag sie jeden.
3. **I live with her.** Ich wohne bei ihr.
4. **Are they coming with us?** Kommen sie mit uns?
5. **I'll call you after the game.** Ich rufe dich nach dem Spiel an.
6. **Since the fall of the wall, Berlin is becoming better.** Seit dem Mauerfall wird Berlin besser.
7. **That gift is from me.** Das Geschenk ist von mir.
8. **Are you going to work?** Gehst du zur Arbeit?
9. **According to the contract, I have to pay 500 Euro.** Gemäß dem Vertrag muss ich 500 Euro bezahlen.
10. **The bank is across from the post office.** Die Bank ist gegenüber von der Post.

Day 46: Two-Way Prepositions, Contractions

These prepositions are called *two-way* because they can either be accusative or dative. All of the two way prepositions show position and location. If the sentence shows motion or a change in state, use accusative. If there is no motion, use dative. Study the following examples:

| I am hanging the photo on the wall. | Ich hänge das Foto an die Wand. |
| The photo is on the wall. | Das Foto ist an der Wand. |

The following prepositions can take either the accusative or dative case:

Two-way Prepositions	
on (vertical)	an
on (horizontal)	auf
behind	hinter
in	in
next to	neben
above	über
under	unter
in front of	vor
between	zwischen

Contractions can be made with certain prepositions and cases. Study the following examples:

Contractions	
an + dem	am
an + das	ans
auf + das	aufs
bei + dem	beim
in + dem	im
in + das	ins
von + dem	vom
zu + dem	zum
zu + der (fem. dat.)	zur

Day 46 Vocabulary

1. **on (vertical surface)** *akk. / dat.* an
2. **on (horizontal surface)** *akk. / dat.* auf
3. **behind** *akk. / dat.* hinter
4. **in** *akk. / dat.* in
5. **next to** *akk. / dat.* neben
6. **above** *akk. / dat.* über
7. **under** *akk. / dat.* unter
8. **in front of** *akk. / dat.* vor
9. **between** *akk. / dat.* zwischen
10. **to hang** hängen |hing, gehangen|

Example Sentences

1. **The picture is on the wall.** Das Bild ist an der Wand.
2. **The plate is on the counter.** Der Teller ist auf der Theke.
3. **I am putting it behind the bed.** Ich stelle es hinter das Bett.
4. **The food is in the refrigerator.** Das Essen ist im Kühlschrank.
5. **We are walking next to the river.** Wir spazieren neben den Fluss.
6. **The ball is flying above my head.** Der Ball fliegt über meinen Kopf.
7. **The cat is under the chair.** Die Katze ist unter dem Stuhl.
8. **The house is in front of me.** Das Haus ist vor mir.
9. **Can you put it between the plants?** Kannst du es zwischen die Pflanzen stellen?
10. **She is hanging the photos on the wall.** Sie hängt die Fotos an die Wand.

Day 47: Genitive Prepositions

There are also genitive prepositions. As mentioned earlier, the genitive case is going out of style, and many people just use the dative case for these propositions.

Genitive Prepositions	
instead of	anstatt / statt
outside of	außerhalb
inside of	innerhalb
despite	trotz
during	während
because of	wegen
beyond	jenseits

Genitive prepositions will be noted *gen.* to remind you that they always use the genitive case.

<u>Day 47 Vocabulary</u>
1. **instead of** *gen.* anstatt / statt
*There is no discernible difference between *anstatt* and *statt*.
2. **outside of** *gen.* außerhalb
3. **inside of** *gen.* innerhalb
4. **despite** *gen.* trotz
5. **during** *gen.* während
6. **because of** *gen.* wegen
7. **beyond** *gen.* jenseits
8. **ready** bereit
9. **together** zusammen
10. **also** auch

<u>Example Sentences</u>
1. **I am eating ham instead of the turkey.** Anstatt des Truthahns esse ich Schinken.
2. **She is standing outside of the house.** Sie steht außerhalb des Hauses.
3. **The country is inside of the EU.** Das Land ist innerhalb der EU.
4. **We are going out despite the bad weather.** Trotz des schlechten Wetters gehen wir aus.
5. **They are talking during the movie.** Sie reden während des Filmes.
6. **I can't come because of my cold.** Wegen meiner Erkältung kann ich nicht kommen.
7. **They are beyond our border.** Sie sind jenseits unserer Grenze.
8. **Are you ready?** Bist du bereit?
9. **We are eating together.** Wir essen zusammen.
10. **I'm coming too!** Ich komme auch!

All of these prepositions can be translated as *to*. The following lesson will explain the differences.

An is used when going up to a border edge, or wall. *Auf* is used when the destination is on top of something. Study the following examples:

I am going to the beach.	Ich gehe an den Strand.
She went to the window.	Sie ging ans Fenster.
I'm going to the toilet.	Ich gehe auf die Toilette.
She is going to the countryside.	Sie fährt aufs Land.

In is used when going into something, and also with countries that have an article. *Nach* is used with countries, cities, or your home, as well as directions like *left* and *right*.

I'm going to bed.	Ich gehe ins Bett.
He is going to the city.	Er geht in die Stadt.
We are traveling to Switzerland.	Wir reisen in die Schweiz.
We are driving to Berlin.	Wir fahren nach Berlin.
I'm going home.	Ich gehe nach Hause.
It goes from left to right.	Es geht von links nach rechts.

For everything else use *zu*. If you can't remember what preposition to use, just use *zu* as your default and a German speaker will understand. *Zu* is also used when going to a person. The phrase *zu Hause* means *at home*. You can often replace *in* with *zu,* which translates that you are going somewhere, but not necessarily into it:

Go to the church.	Geh zur Kirche.
Come to me.	Komm zu mir.
She is going to the train station.	Sie geht zum Bahnhof.

<u>Day 48 Grammar Cards</u>
1. **an (to)**
border / edge / wall
2. **auf (to)**
on top of destination
3. **in (to)**
into / countries with an article
4. **nach (to)**
countries / cities / home / directions
5. **zu (to)**
default / people
6. **at home**
zu Hause

<u>Day 48 Vocabulary</u>
1. **dry cleaner's** die Reinigung (-en)
2. **cathedral** der Dom (-e)
3. **ATM** der Geldautomat (-en)
4. **diner** der Imbiss (-e)
5. **shopping mall** das Einkaufszentrum (die Einkaufszentren)
6. **embassy** die Botschaft (-en)
7. **customs office** das Zollamt (ä, -er)
8. **office** das Büro (-s)
9. **train station** der Bahnhof (ö, -e)
10. **hairdresser** der Friseur (-e) / die Friseurin (-nen)

<u>Example Sentences</u>
1. **I am going to the dry cleaner's.** Ich gehe in die Reinigung.
2. **She went to the cathedral.** Sie ging zum Dom.
3. **He is going to the ATM.** Er geht an den Geldautomaten.
4. **I'm driving to the diner.** Ich fahre zum Imbiss.
5. **We went to the shopping mall.** Wir gingen ins Einkaufszentrum.
6. **I have to go to the embassy.** Ich muss zur Botschaft gehen.
7. **He is in the customs office.** Er ist im Zollamt.
8. **She is in the office.** Sie ist im Büro.
9. **They went to the train station.** Sie gingen zum Bahnhof.
10. **She went to the hairdresser.** Sie ging zum Friseur.

Day 49: Directions

As stated yesterday, the preposition *nach* is used with directions. Study the following examples and notice the different translation for up and down, because *to the up* sounds strange in English:

to the left	nach links
to the right	nach rechts
upward	nach oben
downward	nach unten

To ask for directions, use the phrase *Wie kommt man ~* with the appropriate preposition.

How do you get to the beach?	Wie kommt man an den Strand?	Lit. How does one come to the beach?
How do you get to Switzerland?	Wie kommt man in die Schweiz?	Lit. How does one come to Switzerland?
How do you get to Berlin?	Wie kommt man nach Berlin?	Lit. How does one come to Berlin?

1. **Asking directions**
Wie kommt man ~

Day 49 Vocabulary
1. **left** links
2. **right** rechts
3. **everywhere** überall
4. **nowhere** nirgendwo
5. **somewhere** irgendwo
6. **above** oben
7. **below / at the bottom** unten
8. **to look / glance / peek** gucken
Gucken has a nuance of a quick look.
9. **to look / view** blicken
Blicken has a nuance of *viewing*. The noun *der Blick*, means *the view*.
10. **to look / see** schauen
Schauen has a nuance of *to scan*. The idiom *Mal schauen...* means *We shall see...*

Example Sentences
1. **I'm looking to the left.** Ich gucke nach links.
2. **She is looking to the right.** Sie guckt nach rechts.
3. **I looked everywhere!** Ich habe überall gesucht.
4. **It's nowhere.** Es ist nirgendwo.
5. **It must be somewhere!** Es muss irgendwo sein!
6. **Did you look up above?** Hast du nach oben geschaut?
7. **Did they look down below?** Haben sie nach unten geschaut?
8. **You peeped in the shower!** Du hast in die Dusche geguckt!
9. **I am looking at the mountains.** Ich blicke auf die Berge.
10. **He is looking into the sky.** Er schaut in den Himmel.

Day 50: *Da / Wo* Compounds

In English some people say it's bad form to end a sentence with a preposition. German has found a way around this with da / wo compounds. Da / wo connected to a preposition acts as a sort of nameless pronoun. *Da* is used with statements, *wo* is used with questions. If the preposition starts with a vowel, an *r* will be added as well. *Da / wo* compounds can not take the place of people or relative pronouns. Study the following examples:

I am learning a lot from it.	Ich lerne viel davon.
I will come after (it ends).	Ich komme danach.
What are you waiting for?	Worauf wartest du?
What are you talking about?	Worüber sprichst du?

<u>Day 50 Grammar Card</u>
1. da / wo compounds
Acts as a nameless pronoun.
Use *da* for statements.
Use *wo* for questions.
Add *-r* if preposition starts with vowel.
Can not take the place of people or relative pronouns.

<u>Day 50 Vocabulary</u>
1. to be happy *about* / to look forward *to* sich freuen *auf / über*
*Sich freuen auf means *to look forward to, sich freuen über* means *to be happy about.*
2. to apply *for* sich bewerben *um*
3. to take care *of* sich kümmern *um*
4. to be interested *in* sich interessieren *für*
5. to prepare *for* sich vor'bereiten *auf*
6. to decide *on* sich entscheiden *für* |entschied, entschieden|
7. to pay attention *to* achten *auf*
8. to fight / struggle / compete *for* kämpfen *um*
9. to die *of* sterben *an* (stirbt) |starb, gestorben|
10. to depend *on* ab'hängen *von*
*Abhängen means to depend on, but the phrase *It all depends* is idiomatic in German, and translates to: *Es kommt darauf an.*

<u>Example Sentences</u>
1. Are you looking forward to it? Freust du dich darauf?
2. What are you applying for? Worum bewerben Sie sich?
3. He is taking care of it. Er kümmert sich darum.
4. Are they interested in it? Interessieren sie sich dafür?
5. What is she preparing for? Worauf bereitet sie sich vor?
6. What are you deciding on? Wofür entscheidest du dich?
7. I am paying attention to it. Ich achte darauf.
8. What are you fighting for? Worum kämpfst du?
9. What are we dying of? Woran sterben wir?
10. Everything depends on it. Alles hängt davon ab.

Day 51: Word Order

Like English, basic German word order is subject, verb, object (SVO). You've also learned many ways in which German sends the verb to the end of the sentence. Sentences can be more complex by adding the time (T), manner (M), and place (P). Study the following example:

| I'm going into the city today by car. | Ich fahre heute mit dem Auto in die Stadt. |

Notice the English example uses the order S-V-P-T-M, while the German example uses the order S-V-T-M-P. The default German word order is T-M-P, however, like in English, you can rearrange T-M-P however you like, but your sentence may sound funny or poetic. If you begin a sentence with T, M, or P, S and V will switch places. Study the following example:

| Today I'm going into the city by car. | Heute fahre ich mit dem Auto in die Stadt. |

Sentence structure is a bit more complicated when using a direct object (DO) and an indirect object (IO). In German, the IO will come first. However, if the DO is a pronoun, it will come first. Study the following examples:

I bought my mother the flowers.	Ich kaufte meiner Mutter die Blumen.
I bought the flowers for her.	Ich kaufte ihr die Blumen.
I bought them for my mother.	Ich kaufte sie meiner Mutter.
I bought them for her.	Ich kaufte sie ihr.

To conclude, basic word order is S-V-IO-DO-T-M-P. If the DO is a pronoun, IO and DO are switched. If the sentence starts with T, M, or P, switch S and V.

Day 51 Grammar Cards
1. **Word order**
S-V-IO-DO-T-M-P
S-V-DO-IO-T-M-P (pronoun DO)
(T-M-P) V-S-IO-DO

Day 51 Vocabulary
1. **agency** die Behörde (-n)
2. **often / frequently** häufig
3. **law** das Gesetz (-e)
4. **percentage / share** der Anteil (-e)
5. **solution / answer** die Lösung (-en)
6. **stock / share** die Aktie (-n)
7. **club / association** der Verein (-e)
8. **official document / notice** der Bescheid (-e)
*The phrase *Let me know*, uses this word: *Sag mir Bescheid.*
9. **step** der Schritt (-e)
der Schritt is quite a versatile word. It can literally mean *step* as in *footsteps*, but also has the metaphorical meaning, like: *Let's take a step backward.* An idiomatic expression is *Schitt für Schritt*, which can be translated as: *gradually*, *step by step*.
10. **population / public** die Bevölkerung (-en)

Example Sentences
1. **The agency gave it to me.** Die Behörde gab es mir.
2. **I buy her presents frequently.** Ich kaufe ihr häufig Geschenke.
3. **He explained the law to me.** Er erklärte mir das Gesetz.
4. **He gave his share to her.** Er gab ihr seinen Anteil.
5. **Can you tell me the solution?** Kannst du mir die Lösung verraten?
6. **He sold his shares to the bank.** Er verkaufte der Bank seine Aktien.
7. **The club gave it to him.** Der Verein gab es ihm.
8. **Please give me the official document.** Bitte geben Sie mir den Bescheid.
9. **I'll tell you the dance steps.** Ich bringe dir die Schritte bei.
10. **The public opinion is changing.** Die Meinung der Bevölkerung ändert sich.

Day 52: Relative Clauses and Pronouns

Relative clauses are used to join two sentences together into one. German relative clauses will send the verb to the end. Study the following example:

The man is called David.	Der Mann heißt David.
I am meeting the man in Germany.	Ich treffe den Mann in Deutschland.
The man that I am meeting in Germany is called David.	Der Mann, den ich in Deutschland treffe, heißt David.

German relative pronouns (that / which / who / whose) take their gender from the noun the represent, and their case from the clause they are in. In the previous example, the relative pronoun *den* (that) took its gender from the noun it represented, *Der Mann*, and its case from the second sentence (accusative). Study the following examples:

The woman who I help is nice.	Die Frau, der ich helfe, ist nett.
The child whose toy is broken is crying.	Das Kind, dessen Spielzeug kaputt ist, weint.
The flowers that I am giving you are pretty.	Die Blumen, die ich dir gebe, sind schön.

The relative pronoun grammar table is almost the same as the definite article table, the only differences are in the genitive and dative plural:

Relative Pronouns			
	Masculine	Feminine	Neutral	Plural
Nominative	der	die	das	die
Accusative	den	die	das	die
Dative	dem	der	dem	denen
Genitive	dessen	deren	dessen	deren

Using an accusative, dative, or genitive preposition before the relative pronoun will also change its case. Study the following example:

| The fork with which I am eating is dirty. | Die Gabel, mit der ich esse, ist schmutzig. |

Day 52 Grammar Card
1. **Relative clause and pronouns**
Send verb to end of relative clause.
Gender from main clause, case from relative clause.

Relative Pronouns				
	Masculine	Feminine	Neutral	Plural
Nominative	der	die	das	die
Accusative	den	die	das	die
Dative	dem	der	dem	denen
Genitive	dessen	deren	dessen	deren

Day 52 Vocabulary
1. **fruit** das Obst (no plural)
2. **vegetable** das Gemüse
3. **strawberry** die Erdbeere (-e)
4. **cherry** die Kirsche (-n)
5. **grape** die Traube (-n)
6. **lemon** die Zitrone (-n)
7. **bean** die Bohne (-n)
8. **cucumber** die Gurke (-n)
9. **onion** die Zwiebel (-n)
10. **corn** der Mais

Example Sentences
1. **The fruits that I am buying are delicious.** Das Obst, das ich kaufe, ist lecker.
2. **The vegetable that she is buying is a tomato.** Das Gemüse, das sie kauft, ist eine Tomate.
3. **She is the woman who eats strawberries.** Sie ist die Frau, die Erdbeeren isst.
4. **I have cherries, whose seeds are big.** Ich habe Kirschen, deren Kerne groß sind.
5. **He likes grapes that are green.** Er mag Trauben, die grün sind.
6. **The lemons that we eat are sour.** Die Zitronen, die wir essen, sind sauer.
7. **The people I'm meeting like beans.** Die Leute, mit denen ich mich treffe, mögen Bohnen.
8. **The man she is helping is eating a cucumber.** Der Mann, dem sie hilft, isst eine Gurke.
9. **The onion I am buying smells good.** Die Zwiebel, die ich kaufe, riecht gut.
10. **Corn, whose color is brown, tastes bad.** Mais, dessen Farbe braun ist, schmeckt schlecht.

Day 53: Relative Pronoun Was

There is one more relative pronoun: *was*. *Was* is the relative pronoun for *alles* (everything), *etwas* (something), and *nichts* (nothing). Study the following examples:

I love everything that I do.	Ich liebe alles, was ich mache.
I need something that everyone needs.	Ich brauche etwas, was jeder braucht.
I have nothing that is expensive.	Ich habe nichts, was teuer ist.

Day 53 Grammar Card
1. **Relative pronoun *was***
Used with *alles*, *etwas*, *nichts*.

Day 53 Vocabulary
1. **something / anything** etwas
2. **to recommend** empfehlen (empfiehlt) |empfahl, empfohlen|
3. **to grab** an'greifen |griff an, angegriffen|
4. **to fetch / go and get** holen
5. **to lift** heben |hob, gehoben|
6. **to advise** raten *zu* (rät) |riet, geraten|
7. **to promise** versprechen (verspricht) |versprach, versprochen|
8. **to forget** vergessen (vergisst) |vergaß, vergessen|
9. **to hope *for*** hoffen *auf*
10. **to joke** scherzen

Example Sentences
1. **I need something that everyone needs.** Ich brauche etwas, was jeder braucht.
2. **I recommend nothing that is dangerous.** Ich empfehle nichts, was gefährlich ist.
3. **He grabs everything that he loves.** Er greift alles an, was er liebt.
4. **I am getting something, that is important.** Ich hole etwas, was wichtig ist.
5. **They lift nothing that is heavy.** Sie heben nichts, was schwer ist.
6. **We advise nothing, that is illegal.** Wir raten zu nichts, was illegal ist.
7. **I promise nothing that is impossible.** Ich verspreche nichts, was unmöglich ist.
8. **She forgets everything that is important.** Sie vergisst alles, was wichtig ist.
9. **I hope for something, that is impossible.** Ich hoffe auf etwas, was unmöglich ist.
10. **He jokes about nothing that is complex.** Er scherzt über nichts, was schwierig ist.

Day 54: Subordinating Conjunctions Part 1

Subordinating conjunction is a fancy term for words that are used to combine clauses. Some prepositions also act as conjunctions, but have no impact on the case of the clause. For example *bis* (until) is an accusative preposition, but as a conjunction has no impact. Study the following subordinating conjunctions:

Subordinating Conjunctions	
as / when	als
before	bevor / ehe
until	bis
as / since / because	da
so that / in order to	damit
that	dass
in case	falls
after	nachdem

The clause with the conjunction will send the verb to the end of the sentence, and if the sentence begins with these conjunctions, the verb of the main clause will directly follow the verb of the subordinate clause. Study the following examples:

I'm doing it now so I am prepared tomorrow.	Ich mache es jetzt, damit ich morgen bereit bin.
I'm doing it now so I am prepared tomorrow.	Damit ich morgen bereit bin, mache ich es jetzt.

Unlike English, the conjunction *dass* (that) is used with *wollen* (to want). Study the following example:

I want you to come.	Ich will, dass du kommst.	Lit. I want that you come.

1. **Clauses with *wollen***
Add *dass*.

Day 54 Vocabulary
1. **as / when** als
2. **before** bevor / ehe
*There is no difference between these words. However, *ehe* is less common and is a homonym with the noun *die Ehe* (marriage).
3. **marriage** die Ehe (-n)
4. **until** bis
5. **as / since / because** da
6. **so that / in order to** damit
7. **that** dass
8. **in case** falls
9. **after** nachdem
10. **to save / conserve** sparen

Example Sentences
1. **When I was a child, I was short.** Als ich ein Kind war, war ich klein.
2. **Before I go out, I have to shower.** Bevor ich ausgehe, muss ich duschen.
3. **They annulled their marriage.** Sie haben ihre Ehe anulliert.
4. **I am studying until I know everything.** Ich lerne, bis ich alles weiß.
5. **He can't come, because his car is broken.** Da sein Auto kaputt ist, kann er nicht kommen,
6. **I am hurrying, so that I can leave soon.** Ich beeile mich, damit ich bald weggehen kann.
7. **She doesn't know that he is coming.** Sie weiß nicht, dass er kommt.
8. **I save money, in case I need it later.** Ich spare Geld, falls ich es später brauche.
9. **I call her every day after I get home.** Ich rufe sie jeden Tag an, nachdem ich nach Hause gekommen bin.
10. **I can't conserve water.** Ich kann kein Wasser sparen.

Day 55: Subordinating Conjunctions Part 2

Today's lesson covers the remaining subordinating conjunctions. The differences between conjunctions with the same translation will be covered in a later lesson. Study the following list:

Subordinating Conjunctions	
if / whether	ob
obwohl	although
since / since then	seit / seitdem
as soon as	sobald
because	weil
if / when	wenn
even if	selbst wenn

Day 55 Vocabulary
1. **if / whether** ob
2. **although** obwohl
3. **since (time)** seit / **since then** seitdem
4. **as soon as** sobald
5. **because** weil
6. **if / when** wenn
7. **even if** selbst wenn
8. **again** wieder
9. **enough** genug
10. **exactly** genau

Example Sentences
1. **I don't know, if I will come.** Ich weiß nicht, ob ich kommen werde.
2. **Although he is rich, he is not happy.** Obwohl er reich ist, ist er nicht glücklich.
3. **I've been studying Italian since I came to Italy.** Seit ich nach Italien kam, lerne ich Italienisch.
4. **I go to bed as soon as I get home.** Ich gehe ins Bett, sobald ich nach Hause gekommen bin.
5. **I can't come, because I have no time.** Ich kann nicht kommen, weil ich keine Zeit habe.
6. **When I go to the bar, I drink beer.** Wenn ich in die Kneipe gehe, trinke ich Bier.
7. **Even if I have time, I won't come.** Selbst wenn ich Zeit habe, komme ich nicht.
8. **It won't happen again.** Es soll nicht wieder vorkommen.
9. **Is this enough for you?** Ist dir das genug?
10. **I know exactly what you mean.** Ich weiß genau, was du meinst.

Day 56: Coordinating Conjunctions

Unlike the other conjunctions you have learned, coordinating conjunctions <u>do not</u> send the verb to the end of the clause. The word order <u>doesn't</u> change. Since so many grammar constructions in German send the verb to the end of the clause, it may be easier to remember that these words are the only ones that don't.

Coordinating Conjunctions	
but	aber
but rather	sondern
because	denn
unless·	es sei denn
and	und
either / or	entweder / oder
neither / nor	weder / noch

Sondern is a word that doesn't exist in English, and it's important not to confuse it with *aber* (but). It is used to make a correction. The main clause using *sondern* will always be negative.

It's not blue, but red.	Es ist nicht blau, sondern rot.
I'm not going to Berlin, but Hamburg.	Ich gehe nicht nach Berlin, sondern Hamburg.

Nicht nur... sondern auch is used to say *not only... but also*.

I like not only vanilla, but also chocolate.	Ich mag nicht nur Vanille, sondern auch Schokolade.
I want not only a car, but also a house.	Ich will nicht nur ein Auto, sondern auch ein Haus.

Day 56 Grammar Cards
1. **sondern**
Used to make a correction.
Always used opposite a negative clause.
2. **not only... but also**
nicht nur... sondern auch

Day 56 Vocabulary
1. **but** aber
2. **because** denn
3. **unless** es sei denn
4. **and** und
5. **either / or** entweder / oder
6. **neither / nor** weder / noch
7. **to mean / to think / to opine** meinen
*To say *In my opinion...* use the noun *die Meinung* (opinion) with a possessive pronoun (in the genitive case) and *nach*: *Meiner Meinung nach...* The verb will immediately follow.
8. **to use** benutzen
9. **to visit** besuchen
10. **to choose** aus'wählen

Example Sentences
1. **I think so, but I don't know exactly.** Ich denke schon, aber ich weiß es nicht genau.
2. **I eat vegetables because they are healthy.** Ich esse Gemüse, denn es ist gesund.
3. **You have to come unless you have an exemption.** Sie müssen kommen, es sei denn, Sie haben eine Ausnahme.
4. **I'm drinking and I'm driving a car!** Ich trinke und ich fahre Auto!
5. **I am choosing either red or blue.** Ich wähle entweder rot oder blau.
6. **I am choosing neither red nor blue.** Ich wähle weder rot noch blau.
7. **In my opinion, that is bad.** Meiner Meinung nach ist das schlecht.
8. **I am using a fork.** Ich benutze eine Gabel.
9. **Are you visiting your family?** Besuchst du deine Familie?
10. **They are not choosing that.** Sie wählen das nicht aus.

Day 57: Special Conjunctions

Today's conjunctions are special because they can not only be used to connect clauses, but also in a sentence by themselves. Many of the words have similar meanings and are interchangeable. The differences in nuance will be illustrated in the vocabulary section.

The following conjunctions can all be translated as *because of this / for this reason / that's why*:

deswegen	deshalb	darum	daher

The next set of conjunctions explain the consequence of an action, translating to: *therefore / consequently*:

also	so	folglich	infolgedessen	demnach	insofern

The third set of conjunctions show surprise. They can be translated as *despite this / nevertheless / still*:

trotzdem	dennoch	allerdings	indessen

Again, these conjunctions are special because they don't need to link two clauses. When used to connect clauses, the verb will not go the end, but rather, directly follow the conjunction. Study the following examples:

I have money, for this reason, I'll buy it.	Ich habe Geld, deswegen kaufe ich es. Ich habe Geld. Ich kaufe es deswegen.
She invited me, so I went.	Sie lud mich ein, also ging ich. Sie lud mich ein. Ich ging also.
He fights with his wife, despite this, he loves her.	Er streitet sich mit seiner Frau, trotzdem liebt er sie. Er streitet sich mit seiner Frau. Er liebt sie trotzdem.

1. **because of / for this reason / that's why** deswegen / deshalb / darum / daher
Deswegen is the literal translation: *because of that*. *Deshalb* has a slightly more formal nuance, as in *therefore*. *Darum* is slightly more casual, as in *that's why*. *Daher* has a nuance of deduction from reasoning, as in *from there...*
2. **therefore / so** also / so
3. **consequently / following that** folglich / infolgedessen
4. **according to that / accordingly** demnach
5. **insofar as / in this respect** insofern
6. **despite this** trotzdem
7. **however / meanwhile** indessen
8. **nevertheless** dennoch
9. **indeed / certainly** allerdings
10. **admittedly / in fact / indeed** zwar

Example Sentences
1. **I have money, for this reason, I'll buy it.**
Ich habe Geld, deswegen kaufe ich es.
2. **She invited me, so I went.**
Sie lud mich ein, also ging ich.
3. **The movie was successful, and consequently he became famous.**
Der Film war erfolgreich, und infolgedessen wurde er berühmt.
4. **The regulations are accordingly very strict.**
Die Regelungen sind demnach sehr streng.
5. **I have doubts in this respect.**
Insofern zweifele ich daran.
6. **He fights with his wife, despite this, he loves her.**
Er streitet sich mit seiner Frau, trotzdem liebt er sie.
7. **She offered him a coffee, however, he refused.**
Sie bot ihm einen Kaffee an, er lehnte indessen ab.
8. **The weather is bad, but I am nevertheless coming.**
Das Wetter ist schlecht, aber ich komme dennoch.
9. **That was certainly dumb of you.**
Das war allerdings dumm von dir.
10. **I must admit, I don't play a sport, but I am healthy.**
Ich treibe zwar keinen Sport, aber ich bin gesund.

Day 58: *Da / Weil / Denn, Als / Wenn / Wann*

So far you've learned three ways to say because: *da*, *weil*, and *denn*. *Weil* is the most common usage of *because*, so when in doubt, just use *weil*.

Da has the nuance of *since*. *Denn* has the nuance of *for*. Study the following examples:

I couldn't come, since I had too much to do.	Ich konnte nicht kommen, da ich zu viel zu tun hatte.
I err, for I am human.	Ich irre mich, denn ich bin ein Mensch.

Als, wenn, and *wann* all mean *when*. *Als* is used when talking about the past. *Wann* is used when asking a question about time. *Wenn* is used as the conditional *when / if*. Study the following examples:

When I was a child, I often cried.	Als ich ein Kind war, weinte ich oft.
When are you leaving?	Wann gehst du weg?
When I go to the supermarket, I bring my wallet.	Wenn ich zum Supermarkt gehe, nehme ich meine Geldbörse mit.

It's also easy to confuse *wenn* and *ob*. Both can mean *if*, but *ob* means *if / whether*:

I don't know if I am coming.	Ich weiß nicht, ob ich komme.
When I come, I'll let you know.	Wenn ich komme, sage ich dir bescheid.

Day 58 Vocabulary

1. **to be wrong / make a mistake** sich irren
2. **to cry** weinen
3. **to last (time)** dauern
4. **to discover** entdecken
5. **to invent** erfinden |erfand, erfunden|
6. **to smoke** rauchen
7. **to dance** tanzen
8. **to earn (money)** verdienen
9. **to wash** waschen
10. **to teach** lehren

Example Sentences

1. **I'm sorry, but you are mistaken.** Es tut mir leid, aber Sie irren sich.
2. **The child cries every day.** Das Kind weint jeden Tag.
3. **How long does it last?** Wie lange dauert es?
4. **They are discovering something new.** Sie entdecken etwas Neues.
5. **He is inventing a new computer.** Er erfindet einen neuen Computer.
6. **Do you smoke?** Rauchst du?
7. **She can't dance.** Sie kann nicht tanzen.
8. **Do you earn a lot of money?** Verdienen Sie viel Geld?
9. **I have to wash my laundry.** Ich muss meine Wäsche waschen.
10. **He is teaching German.** Er lehrt Deutsch.

Day 59: Adjective Endings Part 1

In German, every adjective must have an appropriate ending corresponding to the case and gender of the noun it is modifying. As far as being understood, these endings don't mater at all. A German speaker will understand you even if you get every adjective ending completely wrong. There are three types of adjective endings, for the definite article (the), indefinite article (a), and nouns with no article.

Definite article endings are the easiest. Simply add -e or -en to an adjective. Study the following table:

Adjective Endings (Definite Article)				
	Masculine	Feminine	Neutral	Plural
Nominative	-e	-e	-e	-en
Accusative	-en	-e	-e	-en
Dative	-en	-en	-en	-en
Genitive	-en	-en	-en	-en

You can either memorize this table or use a trick: If *the* is plural or changes form, add -en. Otherwise add -e. When adding an ending to adjectives that end with -ig, the G sound becomes voiced. For example, *traurig* becomes *traurige* (trau-ri-geh). Study the following examples:

The blue angel.	Der blaue Engel.
The fat man eats.	Der dicke Mann isst.
The funny child laughs.	Das lustige Kind lacht.
I bought the old apple.	Ich kaufte den alten Apfel.
He knows the young woman.	Er kennt die junge Frau.
He knows the young women.	Er kennt die jungen Frauen.

Day 59 Grammar Card

Adjective Endings (Definite Article)				
	Masculine	Feminine	Neutral	Plural
Nominative	-e	-e	-e	-en
Accusative	-en	-e	-e	-en
Dative	-en	-en	-en	-en
Genitive	-en	-en	-en	-en

Day 59 Vocabulary
1. **fat** dick
2. **thin** dünn
3. **new** neu
4. **old** alt
5. **young** jung
6. **tall / big** groß
7. **short** kurz
8. **long** lang
9. **small** klein
10. **friendly** freundlich

Example Sentences
1. **The fat man eats.** Der dicke Mann isst.
2. **The thin woman doesn't eat.** Die dünne Frau isst nicht.
3. **The child drinks the new juice.** Das Kind trinkt den neuen Saft.
4. **He ate the old cheese.** Er hat den alten Käse gegessen.
5. **He knows the young women.** Er kennt die jungen Frauen.
6. **The tall man was sleeping.** Der große Mann hat geschlafen.
7. **The short table is broken.** Der kurze Tisch ist kaputt.
8. **The long table is old.** Der lange Tisch ist alt.
9. **The small chair is new.** Der kleine Stuhl ist neu.
10. **The friendly people are traveling.** Die freundlichen Leute reisen.

Day 60: Adjective Endings Part 2

Today's lesson covers adjective endings after indefinite articles (a). Study the following table:

Adjective Endings (Indefinite Article)				
	Masculine	Feminine	Neutral	Plural
Nominative	-er	-e	-es	-en
Accusative	-en	-e	-es	-en
Dative	-en	-en	-en	-en
Genitive	-en	-en	-en	-en

Notice anything? It's almost the same as the previous table. German grammar will always convey the gender and case of the noun. If these endings were the same as before, when reading *ein alte Mann* and *ein alte Kind*, you wouldn't be able to immediately know the gender of the noun. Because of this, Germans say *ein alter Mann* and *ein altes Kind*.

The trick to memorizing this table is the same as before, if *ein* changes form, and you know the gender and case of the noun just by looking at *ein*, add *-en*. If you can't tell, then add the appropriate ending. Study the following examples:

A blue angel.	Ein blauer Engel.
A fat man eats.	Ein dicker Mann isst.
A funny child laughs.	Ein lustiges Kind lacht.
I bought an old apple.	Ich kaufte einen alten Apfel.
He knows a young woman.	Er kennt eine junge Frau.
He knows no young women.	Er kennt keine jungen Frauen.

Day 60 Grammar Card

Adjective Endings (Indefinite Article)			
	Masculine	Feminine	Neutral	Plural
Nominative	-er	-e	-es	-en
Accusative	-en	-e	-es	-en
Dative	-en	-en	-en	-en
Genitive	-en	-en	-en	-en

Day 60 Vocabulary

1. **good** gut
2. **evil / bad** böse
3. **bad** schlecht
4. **clever / smart** klug
5. **dumb / stupid / idiotic** dumm / doof / blöd
6. **easy / simple** einfach
7. **hard / difficult** schwer / schwierig
8. **happy** glücklich / zufrieden
*Zufrieden means *happy* as in *satisfied / content*.
9. **sad** traurig
10. **tired** müde
*Müde already ends in *-e*, so you don't need to add another one. The same rule applies to other adjectives that end with *-e*.

Example Sentences

1. **A good child eats vegetables.** Ein gutes Kind isst Gemüse.
2. **An evil child eats chocolate.** Ein böses Kind isst Schokolade.
3. **A bad man travels to Germany.** Ein schlechter Mann reist nach Deustchland.
4. **He is meeting with a clever woman.** Er trifft sich mit einer klugen Frau.
5. **I have a dumb friend.** Ich habe einen dummen Freund.
6. **We passed a simple test.** Wir haben eine einfache Prüfung bestanden.
7. **We didn't pass a difficult test.** Wir haben eine schwere Prüfung nicht bestanden.
8. **A happy child smiled.** Ein glückliches Kind lächelte.
9. **I saw a sad dog.** Ich sah einen traurigen Hund.
10. **The tired woman drank coffee.** Die müde Frau trank Kaffee.

Day 61: Adjective Endings Part 3

The final set of adjective endings are for adjectives with no article. Since there are no articles, the adjective ending itself must convey the case and gender of the noun. Because of this, the endings are the exact same as the *der / die / das* conjugations, with the exception of the genitive masculine and genitive neutral being *-en*.

Adjective Endings (No Article)			
	Masculine	Feminine	Neutral	Plural
Nominative	-er	-e	-es	-e
Accusative	-en	-e	-es	-e
Dative	-em	-er	-em	-en
Genitive	-en	-er	-en	-er

Study the following examples:

Blue angels.	Blaue Engel.
The name is Fat Man.	Der Name ist Dicker Mann.
Funny children laugh.	Lustige Kinder lachen.
Old apple, new apple, I'll eat every apple.	Ob alter Apfel oder neuer Apfel, ich esse jeden Apfel.
Young women don't like him.	Junge Frauen mögen ihn nicht.
German beer is the best.	Deutsches Bier ist das beste.

Day 61 Grammar Card

Adjective Endings (No Article)				
	Masculine	Feminine	Neutral	Plural
Nominative	-er	-e	-es	-e
Accusative	-en	-e	-es	-e
Dative	-em	-er	-em	-en
Genitive	-en	-er	-en	-er

Day 61 Vocabulary
1. **fast / quick** schnell
2. **slow** langsam
3. **strong** stark
4. **weak** schwach
5. **loud** laut
6. **quiet** leise
7. **sweet / cute** süß
*Süß can refer to sweet tastes and also to say someone is cute.
8. **silent** schweigend / still
*Schweigend refers to not talking. *Still* refers to any kind of lack of noise.
9. **strange** seltsam
10. **crazy** verrückt

Example Sentences
1. **Fast trains arrive early.** Schnelle Züge kommen früh an.
2. **Slow trains arrive late.** Langsame Züge kommen spät an.
3. **I refused with strong conviction.** Ich lehnte mit starker Überzeugung ab.
4. **He has weak muscles.** Er hat schwache Muskeln.
5. **Loud music bothers me.** Laute Musik ärgert mich.
6. **I like quiet music.** Ich mag leise Musik.
7. **In Germany there are many cute girls.** In Deutschland gibt es viele süße Mädchen.
8. **This room is silent.** Dieses Zimmer ist still.
9. **I help strange people.** Ich helfe seltsamen Leuten.
10. **Hey crazy man!** Hey verrückter Mann!

Day 62: Comparative and Superlative

The comparative form of adjectives is very similar to English. Add -*er*, plus the appropriate adjective ending. English also uses *more*, but German doesn't, just add -*er*. Study the following examples:

A fatter man.	Ein dickerer Mann.
The fatter man.	Der dickere Mann.
A more beautiful woman.	Eine schönere Frau.
The more beautiful woman.	Die schönere Frau.
A louder child.	Ein lauteres Kind.
The louder child.	Das lautere Kind.

To make the superlative (-*est / the most* ~) add the ending -*st* or -*est* and the appropriate adjective ending. Adjectives that end in *t*, *d*, *s*, or *z* will take -*est*. Study the following examples:

The fattest man.	Der dickste Mann.
The most beautiful woman.	Die schönste Frau.
The loudest child.	Das lauteste Kind.

If no noun follows the adjective, German can add *am* (an + dem) which literally translates to *at the most* ~. This is more often used with verbs other than *sein* (to be), because with *sein* you can simply use a definite article, like English. Notice with *am* the adjective is now in the dative case, and will always add -*en*. Study the following examples:

He is the fattest.	Er ist der dickste. Er ist am dicksten.
She is the most beautiful.	Sie ist die schönste. Sie ist am schönsten.
The child screams the loudest.	Das Kind schreit am lautesten.

1. **Comparative form**
Add *-er* + adjective ending.
2. **Superlative form**
Add *-st* / *-est* (t / d / s / z) + adjective ending
3. **Superlative (No Noun)**
am (adjective) + *-sten* / *-esten* (t / d / s / z)

Day 62 Vocabulary
1. **rich** reich
2. **poor** arm
3. **honest** ehrlich
4. **lonely** einsam
5. **lazy** faul
6. **hard-working** fleißig
7. **dangerous** gefährlich
8. **safe / sure / certain** sicher
9. **pious** fromm
10. **greedy** gierig

Example Sentences
1. **He is the richest.** Er ist am reichsten.
2. **The child is poorer.** Das Kind ist ärmer.
3. **We are more honest.** Wir sind ehrlicher.
4. **I am the loneliest.** Ich bin am einsamsten.
5. **You are lazier.** Du bist fauler.
6. **She is the most hard-working.** Sie ist am fleißigsten.
7. **This is more dangerous.** Das ist gefährlicher.
8. **Here is the safest.** Hier ist es am sichersten.
9. **She is the most pious.** Sie ist am frommsten.
10. **They are greedier.** Sie sind gieriger.

Day 63: Comparisons

German is better than English! Maybe not, but let's learn how to compare two things. To compare two similar things (*as ~ as*), German uses *genauso ~ wie* with positive sentences, and *so ~ wie* with negative sentences. English comparisons use the accusative case for the second word, but German uses the nominative for both sides. Study the following examples:

She is as beautiful as me.	Sie ist genauso schön wie ich.	Lit. She is as beautiful as I.
I am not as fat as him.	Ich bin nicht so dick wie er.	Lit. I am not as fat as he.

To make a comparison with *than*, German uses *als*. Study the following examples:

She is more beautiful than me.	Sie ist schöner als ich.
He is fatter than you.	Er ist dicker als du.

To express a double comparative (*the ~ the ~*), German uses *je ~ desto ~*. Study the following examples:

The bigger the better.	Je größer desto besser.
The more the merrier.	Je mehr desto besser.

<u>Day 63 Grammar Cards</u>
1. **Comparison case**
Both sides nominative.
2. **as ~ as ~**
genauso ~ wie ~
3. **not as ~ as ~**
so ~ wie ~
4. **than (comparisons)**
als
5. **the ~ the ~**
je ~ desto ~

<u>Day 63 Vocabulary</u>
1. **bright** hell
2. **dark** dunkel
3. **wide** breit
4. **narrow** eng
5. **easy** leicht
6. **delicious** lecker
*Adjectives ending in *-el* and *-er* drop *-e* in the comparative form. However, *lecker* does not.
7. **tasteless / unappetizing** geschmacklos
Geschmacklos can refer to food or tasteless behavior.
8. **fashionable** modisch
9. **expensive** teuer
10. **cheap** billig / preiswert

<u>Example Sentences</u>
1. **The inside is brighter than the outside.** Die Innenseite ist heller als die Außenseite.
2. **This picture is darker than that one.** Dieses Bild ist dunkler als jenes Bild.
3. **The wider the easier it is.** Je breiter es ist, desto leichter ist es.
4. **The more narrow the harder it is.** Je enger es ist, desto schwieriger ist es.
5. **My homework is as easy to understand as yours.** Meine Hausaufgabe ist genauso leicht zu verstehen wie deine.
6. **Chocolate is as delicious as vanilla.** Schokolade ist genauso lecker wie Vanille.
7. **Broccoli is as tasteless as cauliflower.** Brokkoli ist genauso geschmacklos wie Blumenkohl.
8. **I am more fashionable than you.** Ich kleide mich modischer als du.
9. **This is more expensive than that other one over there.** Das hier ist teurer als das andere da drüben.
10. **This is cheaper than that.** Das ist billiger als das.

Day 64: Special Comparatives, Would Rather ~

Like English, some adjectives have special comparative forms. English speakers don't say *good gooder goodest*, they say *good better best*. German also has special comparatives. Study the following list:

soon / sooner / soonest	bald / eher / am ehesten
like / more liked / most liked	gern / lieber / am liebsten
good / better / best	gut / besser / am besten
high / higher / highest	hoch / höher / am höchsten
much / more / most	viel / mehr / am meisten

Some adjectives also add an umlaut in their comparative and superlative forms. These adjectives are most often single syllables. Study the following examples:

old / older / oldest	alt / älter / am ältesten
big / bigger / biggest	groß / größer / am größten
clever / cleverer / cleverest	klug / klüger / am klügsten
near / nearer / nearest	nah / näher / am nächsten
rude / ruder / rudest	grob / gröber / am gröbsten
hard / harder / hardest	hart / härter / am härtesten

The phrase *I would rather ~* uses the subjunctive form of *mögen* and the comparative form of *gern*: *Ich möchte lieber ~*. The subjunctive will be covered later, but here is a preview: *mögen* (to like) becomes *möchten* (would like). Study the following examples:

Would you rather eat one or two bananas?	Möchten Sie lieber eine oder zwei Bananen essen?
I would rather eat a Döner Kebab.	Ich möchte lieber einen Döner Kebab essen.

<u>Day 64 Grammar Cards</u>
1. **like / more liked / most liked**
gern / lieber / am liebsten
2. **good / better / best**
gut / besser / am besten
3. **much / more / most**
viel / mehr / am meisten
4. **I would rather...**
Ich möchte lieber...

<u>Day 64 Vocabulary</u>
1. **soon / sooner / soonest** bald / eher / am ehesten
2. **high / higher / highest** hoch / höher / am höchsten
3. **low** niedrig
4. **close** nah
5. **far** weit
6. **polite** höflich
7. **rude / rough** grob / unhöflich
8. **soft** weich
9. **courageous / brave** mutig
10. **cowardly** feig

<u>Example Sentences</u>
1. **I arrived sooner than her.** Ich war eher dort als sie.
2. **Mt. Everest is the highest mountain.** Mt. Everest ist der höchste Berg.
3. **The Dead Sea has the lowest shore.** Das Tote Meer hat die niedrigste Küste.
4. **She is closer than you.** Sie ist näher als du.
5. **You are farther away than her.** Du bist weiter weg als sie.
6. **You all are the most polite.** Ihr seid am höflichsten.
7. **They are the rudest.** Sie sind am gröbsten.
8. **This is the softest pillow.** Dieses Kissen ist das weichste.
9. **He is the bravest man I know.** Er ist der mutigste Mann, den ich kenne.
10. **You are more cowardly than him.** Du bist feiger als er.

Day 65: Verbs as Adjectives

Have you seen the movie The Running Man? It's a classic. Do you see how the verb *to run* acts as an adjective in this title? English adds *-ing* to convert verbs into adjectives. German adds *-d* to the infinitive, and since the verb is now an adjective, remember to add the appropriate adjective ending. Study the following examples:

The running man.	Der laufende Mann.
A running man.	Ein laufender Mann.
The crying child.	Das weinende Kind.
A crying child.	Ein weinendes Kind.
The sleeping woman.	Die schlafende Frau.
A sleeping woman.	Eine schlafende Frau.

To use this grammar with the past tense, simply use the past participle and add the appropriate adjective ending. Study the following examples:

A well read book.	Ein viel gelesenes Buch.
The well read book.	Das viel gelesene Buch.
A lost child.	Ein verirrtes Kind.
The lost child.	Das verirrte Kind.

A note on translation: This grammar can be used interchangeably with relative clauses. Instead of saying *the running man*, you can say, *the man, who runs*. When translating, depending on context, one grammar form might sound more natural than the other.

1. **Verb → Adjective (present tense)**
Add -*d* + adjective ending.
2. **Verb → Adjective (past tense)**
(past participle) + adjective ending.

Most of today's words have a male and female version. Remember, female versions add -*in*.

Day 65 Vocabulary
1. **guy / fellow / type** der Typ (-en)
2. **dude / guy / man** der Kerl (-e)
3. **friend / boyfriend / girlfriend** der Freund (-e) / die Freundin (-nen)
4. **buddy / pal** der Bekannte (-n) / die Bekannte (-n)
5. **co-worker / colleague** der Kollege (-n) / die Kollegin (-nen)
6. **enemy** der Feind (-e) / die Feindin (-nen)
7. **boss** der Chef (-s) / die Chefin (-nen)
8. **neighbor** der Nachbar (-n) / die Nachbarin (-nen)
9. **roommate** der Mitbewohner / die Mitbewohnerin (-nen)
10. **classmate** der Mitschüler / die Mitschülerin (-nen)

Example Sentences
1. **The sleeping guy is lazy.** Der schlafende Typ ist faul.
2. **The drinking dude is over there.** Der trinkende Kerl ist da drüben.
3. **I need a thinking friend.** Ich brauche einen denkenden Freund.
4. **My crying buddy is sad.** Mein weinender Bekannter ist traurig.
5. **The hard-working colleagues go home early.** Die fleißigen Kollegen gehen früh nach Hause.
6. **Her dying enemy cursed.** Ihr sterbender Feind fluchte.
7. **The yelling boss can't calm down.** Der schreiende Chef kann sich nicht beruhigen.
8. **The TV watching neighbor pays his rent.** Der fernsehende Nachbar bezahlt seine Miete.
9. **My good looking roommate cooks.** Mein gut aussehender Mitbewohner kocht.
10. **A studying classmate falls asleep.** Eine lernende Mitschülerin schläft ein.

Day 66: Adjectives as Nouns

At a bar you might hear the phrase, "I'll take a cold one." In English, to make an adjective into a noun, words like *one, thing, man, woman* are added. German doesn't require this and can simply use the adjective. However, you must add the adjective ending based on the noun being represented. Study the following example:

I'll take a cold one.	Ich nehme ein Kaltes.

Notice *one*, which represents *beer*, is omitted in German, and *Kaltes* is capitalized because it became a noun. The adjective ending *-es* comes from the accusative neutral *das Bier*.

To illustrate this further, think of the movie *The Good, the Bad, and the Ugly*. If the title was referring to a good man, a bad man, and an ugly man, the title would be: *Der Gute, der Böse, und der Hässliche*. However, if the title was referring to the idea or concept of good, bad, and ugly idealism, it would be *Das Gute, das Böse, und das Hässliche*. Because of this confusion, the title in German is actually *Zwei glorreiche Halunken* (Two Glorious Scoundrels). Apparently the third guy was lost in translation.

Day 66 Vocabulary
1. **ambitious** ehrgeizig
2. **cruel / terrible** grausam
3. **pleasant / agreeable** angenehm
4. **generous / noble** großherzig
5. **modest / humble** bescheiden
6. **moody / cranky** launisch
7. **proud** stolz
8. **reliable / dependable** zuverlässig
9. **stubborn** stur
10. **comical / weird / strange** komisch
Komisch is a bit different than *comical*. You can use it to mean funny, but only if that thing is funny because it is strange. If something is funny use *lustig* or *witzig*.

Example Sentences
1. **The ambitious ones achieve more.** Die Ehrgeizigen erreichen mehr.
2. **He is a really cruel one.** Er ist ein ganz Grausamer.
3. **He is a pleasant one.** Er ist ein Angenehmer.
4. **The generous ones are friendly.** Die Großherzigen sind freundlich.
5. **I don't know even one modest one.** Ich kenne keinen einzigen Bescheidenen.
6. **She is a moody one.** Sie ist eine Launische.
7. **The proud often have a weakness.** Die Stolzen haben oft eine Schwachstelle.
8. **I need a dependable one.** Ich brauche einen Zuverlässigen.
9. **The billy goat is really a stubborn one.** Der Ziegenbock ist echt ein Sturer.
10. **The comedian is really a comical one.** Der Komiker ist ein ganz Komischer.

Day 67: Adjective Practice

Now that you've learned all the basics of adjectives, use these next few lessons to review and practice everything you have learned.

Day 67 Vocabulary
1. **nice** nett
2. **mean** gemein
3. **cute** hübsch
4. **attractive** attraktiv
5. **ugly** hässlich
6. **funny** lustig
7. **boring** langweilig
8. **hot** heiß
9. **cold** kalt
10. **wonderful** wunderbar

Example Sentences
1. **They are nice.** Sie sind nett.
2. **He is mean.** Er ist gemein.
3. **He is a cute child.** Er ist ein hübsches Kind.
4. **She is attractive.** Sie ist attraktiv.
5. **It is an ugly thing.** Es ist ein hässliches Ding.
6. **You all are the funniest.** Ihr seid am lustigen.
7. **I am boring.** Ich bin langweilig.
8. **I'm hot.** Mir ist heiß.
9. **She is cold.** Ihr ist kalt.
10. **You are wonderful.** Du bist wunderbar.

Day 68: Adjective Practice

<u>Day 68 Vocabulary</u>
1. **completely / totally** ganz
2. **probably** wahrscheinlich
3. **else / otherwise** sonst
4. **there** dort / da
*The difference between these words is largely regional. In south west Germany they tend to say *dort* over *da*. Some also use *da* in place of *hier* (here). In this sense, *da* can be used to indicate that something is near the speaker, while *dort* is used to indicate something is away from the speaker. Some speakers favor *dort* when referring to places, like a city or region.
5. **only / simply** nur
6. **always** immer
7. **never** nie
8. **even** sogar
9. **hardly** kaum
10. **almost** fast

<u>Example Sentences</u>
1. **That is really great.** Das ist ganz toll.
2. **I am probably coming today.** Ich komme wahrscheinlich heute.
3. **You have to pay, or it won't work.** Du musst bezahlen, sonst geht es nicht.
4. **She is there, on the sofa.** Sie ist dort / da, auf dem Sofa.
5. **I only love you!** Ich liebe nur dich!
6. **I always eat vegetables!** Ich esse immer Gemüse!
7. **I never eat junk food.** Ich esse nie Junkfood.
8. **Even a child can do that!** Sogar ein Kind kann das!
9. **I hardly drink beer.** Ich trinke kaum Bier.
10. **We are almost there.** Wir sind fast da.

Day 69: Adjective Practice

<u>Day 69 Vocabulary</u>
1. **especially** besonders
2. **actually** eigentlich
3. **finally** endlich
4. **future** die Zukunft (ü, -e)
5. **past** die Vergangenheit (-en)
6. **present** die Gegenwart (-en)
7. **usually / ordinarily** gewöhnlich
8. **normally** normalerweise
9. **mostly** meistens
10. **luckily / fortunately** glücklicherweise

<u>Example Sentences</u>
1. **I especially like sausages.** Ich mag besonders Würstchen.
2. **Actually, I can't go.** Eigentlich kann ich nicht kommen.
3. **I finally passed the test!** Endlich habe ich die Prüfung bestanden!
4. **She looks forward to the future.** Sie freut sich auf die Zukunft.
5. **She has forgotten the past.** Sie hat die Vergangenheit vergessen.
6. **She lives in the present.** Sie lebt in der Gegenwart.
7. **They drink ordinary beer.** Sie trinken gewöhnliches Bier.
8. **They normally drink a lot.** Sie trinken normalerweise viel.
9. **They mostly drink German beer.** Sie trinken meistens deutsches Bier.
10. **Fortunately, they always pay their bill.** Glücklicherweise bezahlen sie immer ihre Rechnung.

Day 70: In Order to, Without Doing, *Man, Lassen, Je*

The next few lessons cover some grammar points that didn't really fit into the other lessons. It's a plethora of information!

To express *in order to ~* in German, use *um ~ zu ~* , with the object coming between *um* and *zu,* and the verb coming after *zu*. If you use a verb with a separable prefix, *zu* goes in between. Study the following examples:

You must study in order to pass the test.	Du musst lernen, um die Prüfung zu bestehen.
She is wearing a dress in order to look gut.	Sie trägt ein Kleid, um gut auszusehen.

To express *without doing,* use *ohne ~ zu ~*. Study the following examples:

You can't pass the test without studying.	Du kannst die Prüfung nicht bestehen, ohne zu lernen.
She spoke to me without looking at him.	Sie sprach mit mir, ohne ihn auszusehen.

German uses the word *man* to mean *one, a person, a human*. English usually uses the word *you* or *one* to refer to an unnamed person. Study the following examples:

One shouldn't do such things.	Solche Dinge sollte man nicht tun.
You might think otherwise.	Man denkt vielleicht anders.

The verb *lassen* means *to let*, or *to allow*. It can also be translated as *leave*. Study the following examples:

Let it be.	Lass es sein.
They won't allow that.	Das lassen sie nicht.
Leave me alone.	Lass mich allein.

Je translates as *ever* or *per,* and is used to ask about experiences, as in: *Have you ever...?* To say that you have never done something, add *noch nie*. Study the following examples:

Have you ever drunk German beer?	Hast du je deutsches Bier getrunken?
Yes I have.	Ja, habe ich.
Have you ever traveled to Berlin?	Bist du je nach Berlin gereist?
I haven't traveled to Berlin.	Ich bin noch nie nach Berlin gereist.

1. **in order to** ~

um ~ zu ~

2. **without ~ing**

ohne ~ zu ~

3. **ever / per**

je

4. **not yet (experiences)**

noch nie

Day 70 Vocabulary

1. **bad luck / misfortune** das Pech
2. **clear** klar

Klar can be used to check for understanding just like in English. *Ist das klar?* (Is that clear?) There are also the idiomatic phrases: *Alles klar!* (All right! / Okay!) and *Na klar!* (Sure! / Of course!).

3. **to let / allow** lassen (lässt) |ließ, gelassen|
4. **possible** möglich
5. **crowd / large amount** die Menge (-n)
6. **flat / level / even** eben
7. **hangover** der Kater

*This word literally means male cat, usually wild, like *tomcat* in English, but is used more often as a slang to say that you have a hangover.

8. **one / person / human** man
9. **runny nose** der Schnupfen

*In the dictionary, this word is first listed as *cold*, but refers to the symptoms in your nose that result from a cold, rather than other symptoms like a headache or coughing.

10. **to finish talking / to make excuses** aus'reden

*This is often used to say *Let me finish talking*, as well as used to make the noun: die Ausrede (-n) (an excuse). However, if you want to use the verb *to make excuses*, change *aus'reden* to *heraus'reden*.

Example Sentences

1. **That's such a shame!** So ein Pech!
2. **Is that clear?** Ist das klar?
3. **They are letting you speak.** Sie lassen dich sprechen.
4. **Everything is possible!** Alles ist möglich!
5. **We have plenty of food.** Wir haben eine Menge Essen.
6. **This table is not level.** Dieser Tisch ist nicht eben.
7. **Have you ever had a hangover?** Hast du je einen Kater gehabt?
8. **One can't do such things.** Solche Dinge kann man nicht machen.
9. **He needs to sleep in order to cure his runny nose.** Er muss schlafen, um seinen Schnupfen auszukurieren.
10. **Let me finish speaking without interrupting.** Lass mich ausreden, ohne zu unterbrechen.

Day 71: *Egal, die Lust, Doch, Ab Sofort*

The word *egal* is translated in the dictionary as *equal* or *whatever*. These translations don't really do the word justice. *Egal* can be used with pronouns in the dative case to say that you don't care about something, or to say that something doesn't matter. Study the following examples:

I don't care about that.	Das ist mir egal.
She doesn't care about the environment.	Umweltschutz ist ihr egal.
That doesn't matter.	Das ist egal.

The word *die Lust* translates as *desire*, and it is used with *haben* to show your desire to do something, literally saying: *I have desire to ~*. It can be translated as: *feel like* or *want*. Study the following examples:

I don't feel like eating. **I don't want to eat.**	Ich habe keine Lust zu essen.
Do you feel like drinking a beer? **Do you want to drink a beer?**	Hast du Lust ein Bier zu trinken?
She feels like going out. **She wants to go out.**	Sie hat Lust auszugehen.

Doch is used to contradict a negative sentence, to say that the opposite is true. It translates to: *but / still / however / yet / actually.* Study the following conversation:

A: You don't like pasta, do you? **B: Actually I do.** **A: But you didn't eat it yesterday.** **B: The pasta yesterday tasted bad,** **but I actually like pasta.**	A: Du magst keine Nudeln, oder? B: Doch. A: Gestern hast du sie aber nicht gegessen. B: Die Nudeln gestern schmeckten nicht gut, doch eigentlich mag ich Nudeln.

Ab ~ bis ~ is used with time to say *from ~ to ~*. *Ab* is often paired with *sofort* (at once / immediately). Study the following examples:

From 10:00 until 14:00.	Ab 10:00 bis 14:00
From now on. **As of now.** **With immediate effect.**	Ab sofort.

<u>Day 71 Grammar Cards</u>
1. **don't care about ~ / ~ doesn't matter**
~ (sein) + (dative pronoun) + egal
2. **feel like ~ing / have desire to ~**
(haben) + Lust + zu ~
3. **but / still / yet / however / actually (contradictions)**
doch
4. **from ~ until ~**
ab ~ bis ~
5. **from now on / as of now / with immediate effect**
ab sofort

<u>Day 71 Vocabulary</u>
1. **doctor** der Arzt (ä, -e) / die Ärztin (-nen)
2. **accountant** der Buchhalter / die Buchhalterin (-nen)
3. **businessman / businesswoman** der Geschäftsmann (ä, -er) / die Geschäftsfrau (-en)
4. **carpenter** der Tischler / die Tischlerin (-nen)
5. **cashier** der Kassierer / die Kassiererin (-nen)
6. **nurse** der Krankenpfleger / die Krankenschwester (-n)
7. **fire fighter** der Feuerwehrmann (ä, -er) / die Feuerwehrfrau (-en)
8. **construction worker** der Bauarbeiter
9. **lawyer** der Anwalt (ä, -e) / die Anwältin (-nen)
10. **writer** der Schriftsteller / die Schriftstellerin (-nen)

<u>Example Sentences</u>
1. **I don't care about what the doctor says.** Mir ist egal, was der Arzt sagt.
2. **Do you want to talk to the accountant?** Hast du Lust mit dem Buchhalter zu sprechen?
3. **I hate business, but I am a businessman.** Ich hasse das Geschäft aber ich bin doch ein Geschäftsmann.
4. **As of now, the carpenter is quitting.** Der Tischler kündigt ab sofort.
5. **The cashier has no desire to work.** Die Kassiererin hat keine Lust zu arbeiten.
6. **The nurse took care of me.** Der Krankenpfleger pflegte mich.
7. **The fire fighter extinguished the fire.** Der Feuerwehrmann löschte das Feuer.
8. **The construction worker is busy.** Der Bauarbeiter ist beschäftigt.
9. **The lawyer doesn't care about the trial.** Der Prozess ist dem Anwalt egal.
10. **From now on, the writer will write.** Ab sofort wird die Schriftstellerin schreiben.

Day 72: *Naja, Tja, Ach So*

Naja is used to indicate that you are thinking, and also when something regrettable happens to say: *oh well*. Another word used when thinking is *tja*. However, this word can not be translated as *oh well*. Study the following examples:

Well, I'm not sure.	Naja, ich bin mir nicht sicher.
It broke? Oh well...	Es hat sich gebrochen? Naja...
Well, I'm not sure.	Tja, ich bin mir nicht sicher.

When listening to someone, and you want to let them know that you are listening and understanding, use the phrase *ach so*. This can be translated as: *Oh I see* or *Oh really?*. Study the following example:

| Oh really? I didn't know that. | Ach so. Das habe ich nicht gewusst. |

Day 72 Vocabulary
1. **caution / attention** die Vorsicht
2. **to find out** *about* / **experience** erfahren *von* (erfährt) |erfuhr, erfahren|
3. **vicinity / proximity / nearby** die Nähe
4. **to commit suicide** sich um'bringen |brachte um, umgebracht|
5. **necessarily / absolutely** unbedingt
*If you really want to do something, use *unbedingt tun wollen,* translating to: *I've been dying to ~*.
6. **power** die Macht (ä, -e)
7. **moment / instant** der Augenblick (-e)
8. **oh well / umm... / well...** naja
9. **well...** tja
10. **Oh I see. / Oh really?** ach so

Example Sentences
1. **I throw caution to the wind.** Ich schlage alle Vorsicht in den Wind.
2. **I found out about your mother's death.** Ich erfuhr vom Tod deiner Mutter.
3. **Is there a bank nearby?** Gibt es eine Bank in der Nähe?
4. **He commit suicide.** Er brachte sich um.
5. **That is not necessarily true.** Das ist nicht unbedingt wahr.
6. **He wants to come to power.** Er will an die Macht kommen.
7. **Please wait a moment.** Bitte warten Sie einen Augenblick.
8. **Umm, well, I think that is a bad idea.** Naja, ich denke, dass das keine gute Idee ist.
9. **Well, I'm not sure.** Tja, ich bin nicht sicher.
10. **Oh I see, that's interesting.** Ach so, das ist ja interessant.

Day 73: Subjunctive: *Konjunktiv II* Part 1

In English, this grammar is called the Subjunctive. In German it is called *Konjunktiv II*. If you don't like grammar terminology, just think about this as hypothetical sentences with *would*. There is a lot to learn here, so this grammar is going to be split up into a few lessons. First, let's learn how to say *would*. German uses the past tense of *werden* with an umlaut. Like modal verbs, the *ich* and *er / sie / es* conjugations are the same. Study the following conjugation:

werden (Konjunktiv II)			
ich	würde	wir	würden
du	würdest	ihr	würdet
er	würde	sie	würden
sie	würde	Sie	würden
es	würde		

To make a hypothetical sentence, use the *Konjunktiv II* of *werden* and the infinitive of the verb, which goes to the end of the sentence. Study the following examples:

I would go.	Ich würde gehen.
He would eat everything.	Er würde alles essen.
We would sleep every day.	Wir würden jeden Tag schlafen.

Do you remember using *gern* to say you like doing something? You can also add *würde* to politely say that you *would like to ~*. Study the following examples:

I would like to go.	Ich würde gern gehen.
He would like to eat everything.	Er würde gern alles essen.
We would like to sleep every day.	Wir würden gern jeden Tag schlafen.

1. **would (verb)**

(würden) + end of sentence (infinitive)

2. **would like (polite)**

(würden) + gern

Day 73 Vocabulary

1. **to argue / fight** streiten |stritt, gestritten|
2. **to play sports** Sport treiben |trieb, getrieben|
3. **to kick / step / tread** treten (tritt) |trat, getreten|
4. **to leave / abandon** verlassen (verlässt) |verließ, verlassen|
5. **to throw** werfen (wirft) |warf, geworfen|
6. **to smell *like*** riechen *nach* |roch, gerochen|
7. **to run** rennen |rannte, gerannt|

Laufen and *rennen* can both be translated as *to run*. However, *laufen* just means movement of your legs, and can also translate as *walking*. *Rennen* can only be used when you are moving quickly.

8. **to laugh *at / about*** lachen *über*
9. **to fantasize** fantasieren *von*
10. **to deliver** aus'tragen (trägt aus) |trug aus, ausgetragen|

Example Sentences

1. **He would argue with anyone.** Er würde mit jedem streiten.
2. **I would like to play sports.** Ich würde gern Sport treiben.
3. **I would like to kick him.** Ich würde ihn gern treten.
4. **Would you abandon your parents?** Würdest du deine Eltern verlassen?
5. **We wouldn't throw it.** Wir würden es nicht werfen.
6. **You all would smell like flowers.** Ihr würdet nach Blumen riechen.
7. **Would you run quickly?** Würden Sie schnell rennen?
8. **What would you laugh about?** Worüber würdest du lachen?
9. **She would fantasize about the future.** Sie würde von der Zukunft fantasieren.
10. **The postman would like to deliver the letters.** Der Briefträger würde gern die Briefe austragen.

To express hypothetical sentences, *würden* doesn't have to be used. Each verb has a Konjunktiv II conjugation! To conjugate verbs into the Konjunktiv II, use the simple past, and add an umlaut to the first vowel where possible. Verbs with *e* and *i* as the first vowel can't add an umlaut, and so their Konjunktiv II is the same as the simple past. Strong verbs also add an *-e* to the conjugations except for *wir / sie / Sie*. Study the following conjugations:

sein (simple past)				sein (Konjunktiv II)			
ich	war	wir	waren	ich	wäre	wir	wären
du	warst	ihr	wart	du	wärest	ihr	wäret
er	war	sie	waren	er	wäre	sie	wären
sie	war	Sie	waren	sie	wäre	Sie	wären
es	war			es	wäre		

haben (simple past)				haben (Konjunktiv II)			
ich	hatte	wir	hatten	ich	hätte	wir	hätten
du	hattest	ihr	hattet	du	hättest	ihr	hättet
er	hatte	sie	hatten	er	hätte	sie	hätten
sie	hatte	Sie	hatten	sie	hätte	Sie	hätten
es	hatte			es	hätte		

gehen (simple past)				gehen (Konjunktiv II)			
ich	ging	wir	gingen	ich	ginge	wir	gingen
du	gingst	ihr	gingt	du	gingest	ihr	ginget
er	ging	sie	gingen	er	ginge	sie	gingen
sie	ging	Sie	gingen	sie	ginge	Sie	gingen
es	ging			es	ginge		

Some words are especially irregular in Konjunktiv II. Instead of using *ä* they will use *ü,* or both. Don't worry too much about memorizing these, the chance that you will encounter them is very rare. Study the following examples:

Infinitive	Simple Past	Konjunktiv II
stehen	stand	stände / stünde
sterben	starb	stürbe
verderben	verdarb	verdürbe

The Konjunktiv II is less common in spoken German. Most people will use the *würde* construction when speaking. Study the following examples with both constructions:

I would go.	Ich würde gehen. Ich ginge.
He would eat that.	Er würde das essen. Er **äße das.**
We would sleep.	Wir würden schlafen. Wir schliefen.

The Konjunktiv II of *sein, haben,* and *mögen* are very common. The latter two especially when making polite requests. Study the following examples:

That would be fine.	Das wäre schön.
I would like to have a Döner Kebab.	Ich hätte gern einen Döner Kebab.
I would like a Döner Kebab.	Ich möchte einen Döner Kebab.

1. **Konjunktiv II**

Simple past + umlaut where possible.

Strong verbs add -*e*.

2. **Konjunktiv II of *stehen*, *sterben*, *verderben***

stände / stünde, stürbe, verdürbe

Day 74 Vocabulary

1. **to perish / disappear / go down** unter'gehen |ging unter, untergegangen|
2. **to lick** lecken
3. **to send** senden |sandte / sendete, gesandt / gesendet|

Senden is a rare word that has multiple spellings. In the 1990s, Germany went through a spelling reform, which changed the spelling of many words. For example, some words now use *ss* instead of *ß*. If you are reading things written prior to 1990, you may find many words spelled differently. *Senden* never decided which spelling to use. For most all cases, you can use either one. However, if you are sending something in a technological sense, like a signal, use the weak form: *sendete / gesendet.*

4. **to pronounce / enunciate** aus'sprechen (spricht aus) |sprach aus, ausgesprochen|
5. **to avenge** rächen
6. **to decay / corrupt** verderben (verdirbt) |verdarb, verdorben|
7. **to excite / stimulate** an'regen
8. **to glow / flash** leuchten
9. **to hunt / chase** jagen
10. **to confuse** verwirren

Example Sentences

1. **If the levee breaks, would the city perish?** Wenn der Damm bräche, ginge die Stadt unter?
2. **Would you lick an old ice cream cone?** Lecktest du eine alte Eistüte?
3. **I would send it tomorrow.** Ich sendete es morgen.
4. **How would you pronounce this?** Wie sprächen Sie das aus?
5. **If I died, would you avenge me?** Wenn ich stürbe, rächtest du mich?
6. **This would decay quickly without water.** Ohne Wasser verdürbe das schnell.
7. **This reaction would excite the atoms.** Diese Reaktion regte die Atome an.
8. **If I lit this, would it glow?** Wenn ich dieses anzündete, leuchtete es?
9. **If he ran, would you chase him?** Wenn er rennte, jagten Sie ihn?

Rennen has an irregular Konjunktiv II, *rennte* instead of *rännte*.

10. **Why would you confuse me?** Warum verwirrtest du mich?

Day 75: Subjunctive: *Konjunktiv II* Part 3

Like other verbs, the Konjunktiv II of modal verbs is the same as the simple past, but umlauts are only added if the infinitive also has an umlaut. Study the following list:

Infinitive	Simple Past	Konjunktiv II
wollen	wollte	wollte
sollen	sollte	sollte
müssen	musste	müsste
dürfen	durfte	dürfte
können	konnte	könnte
mögen	mochte	möchte

Note that since *wollen* and *sollen* have the same simple past and Konjunktiv II, sentences can have two possible translations. You should be able to understand which in context. Study the following example:

I wanted to go. I would want to go.	Ich wollte gehen.

Also note that directly translating the Konjunktiv II of *sollen* (would shall) makes no sense in English, so a better translation, depending on context, is *ought to* or *be supposed to*. Study the following example:

I ought to go. I am supposed to go.	Ich sollte gehen,

Have you heard the famous slang phrase *shoulda woulda coulda* (should have would have could have)? To make a modal verb sentence with this grammar, German uses the Konjunktiv II of *haben* and then a double infinitive of the main verb and the modal verb at the end of the sentence. Study the following examples:

I should have gone to the supermarket.	Ich hätte zum Supermarkt gehen sollen.
We would have wanted to buy it.	Wir hätten es kaufen wollen.
He could have eaten everything. He would have been able to eat everything.	Er hätte alles essen können.

<u>Day 75 Grammar Cards</u>
1. **Konjunktiv II modal verbs without umlaut**
sollen / wollen
2. **Konjunktiv II modal verbs with (haben)**
hätten + end of sentence (main infinitive) + (modal infinitive)

<u>Day 75 Vocabulary</u>
1. **to serve** *dat.* dienen
2. **to dodge** *dat.* aus'weichen |wich aus, ausgewichen|
3. **to notice** bemerken
4. **to turn / rotate** drehen
Drehen takes an object. To turn oneself, use *sich drehen*.
5. **to prove** beweisen |bewies, bewiesen|
6. **to pack** packen
Packen can also add the separable prefix *ein-* to mean *wrap* or *pack up*, or *aus-* to mean *unpack* or *unwrap*.
7. **to increase** erhöhen
8. **to decrease** verringern
9. **to demand / require** fordern
10. **to accompany / escort** begleiten

<u>Example Sentences</u>
1. **I was supposed to serve them.** Ich sollte ihnen dienen.
2. **He couldn't have dodged the bullets.** Er hätte den Kugeln nicht ausweichen können.
3. **She should have noticed it.** Sie hätte es bemerken sollen.
4. **We would like to turn the wheel.** Wir möchten das Rad drehen.
5. **They should have proved it.** Sie hätten es beweisen sollen.
6. **I should have packed my bags.** Ich hätte meine Koffer packen sollen.
7. **Would we be able to increase it?** Könnten wir es erhöhen?
8. **Would we have to decrease it?** Müssten wir es verringern?
9. **They couldn't have demanded that.** Sie hätten das nicht fordern können.
10. **She should have accompanied him.** Sie hätte ihn begleiten sollen.

Day 76: Subjunctive: *Konjunktiv II* Part 4

Hypothetical sentences in the past will use the same grammar as the Perfekt (present perfect), but will use the Konjunktiv II of *sein* or *haben* instead of the present tense. Compare the following examples:

I went.	Ich bin gegangen.
I would have gone.	Ich wäre gegangen.
He ate that.	Er hat das gegessen.
He would have eaten that.	Er hätte das gegessen.

This grammar is mostly used in sentences with *if*. Study the following examples:

If I had gone, I would have died!	Wenn ich gegangen wäre, wäre ich gestorben!
If I had eaten that, I would have had a stomach ache.	Wenn ich das gegessen hätte, hätte ich Bauchschmerzen gehabt.

When translating from English to German, it's important to note that English makes no distinction between past tense and subjunctive verbs, but German does. If you just directly translate, your translation will be incorrect. So remember to use the Konjunktiv II for hypothetical sentences. Study the following example:

If I had eaten that...	(correct) Wenn ich das gegessen hätte...
	(incorrect) Wenn ich das gegessen hatte...

Day 76 Grammar Card
1. **Konjunktiv II (past tense)**
(wären / hätten) + past participle

Day 76 Vocabulary
1. **to continue** fort'fahren (fährt fort) |fuhr fort, fortgefahren|
2. **to climb / ascend** steigen |stieg, gestiegen|
3. **to sell** verkaufen
4. **to change / revise** ändern
5. **to change completely / convert** verändern
*Both *ändern* and *verändern* take objects. To change oneself, use *sich*.
6. **to deliver / provide** liefern
7. **to repeat** wiederholen
8. **to burn** brennen |brannte, gebrannt|
9. **to draw** zeichnen
10. **to converse** sich unterhalten (unterhält) |unterhielt, unterhalten|

Example Sentences
1. **I would have continued, but I couldn't.** Ich wäre fortgefahren, aber ich konnte nicht.
2. **The prices would have climbed even higher.** Die Preise wären noch höher gestiegen.
3. **Would she have sold it?** Hätte sie es verkauft?
4. **I would have liked to revise my essay.** Ich hätte meinen Aufsatz ändern wollen.
5. **I would have liked to change my appearance.** Ich hätte mein Aussehen verändern wollen.
6. **They wouldn't have delivered the mail.** Sie hätten die Post nicht geliefert.
7. **I would have repeated that.** Ich hätte das wiederholt.
8. **Would it have burned?** Hätte es gebrannt?
9. **He would have drawn it.** Er hätte es gezeichnet.
10. **I wouldn't have conversed with him.** Ich hätte mich nicht mit ihm unterhalten.

Day 77: Passive Voice Part 1

If you can't remember your English grammar lessons from high school, the passive voice is used to turn the object into the subject. Instead of saying *I eat the doughnut*, the passive construction: *The doughnut is eaten (by me)*. The construction of the passive voice in German is the same as English, but instead of using *to be* (sein) as the auxiliary verb, Germans use *to become* (werden). Instead of *by,* German uses *von* for animate (living) things and *durch / mit* for inanimate things. Remember that German sentences can take multiple tenses without changing. *Ich esse* can mean: *I eat, I am eating, I do eat.* Similarly, the passive voice has two tenses. Study the following examples:

The doughnut is (being) eaten by me.	Der Donut wird von mir gegessen.
The coffee is (being) made by the coffee maker.	Der Kaffee wird mit die Kaffeemaschine gemacht.

Modal verbs take the spot of *werden*, and will move it to the end of the sentence.

The doughnut can be eaten.	Der Donut kann gegessen werden.
The coffee must be made.	Der Kaffee muss gemacht werden.

To make a past tense passive sentence, simply use the past tense of *werden* or the modal. Study the following examples:

The doughnut was (being) eaten.	Der Doughnut wurde gegessen.
The coffee was (being) made.	Der Kaffee wurde gemacht.
The doughnut could be eaten.	Der Donut konnte gegessen werden.
The coffee had to be made.	Der Kaffee musste gemacht werden.

1. **Passive voice**
(werden) + (past participle)
2. **Modal passive**
(modal) + (past participle) + werden
3. **by (passive)**
von (animate)
durch / mit (inanimate)

Day 77 Vocabulary
1. **to judge** verurteilen
2. **to occupy** besetzen
3. **to fold** falten
4. **to conquer** erobern
5. **to convince / persuade** überzeugen
6. **to bite** beißen |biss, gebissen|
7. **to protect** beschützen
8. **to admit / acknowledge** zu'geben (gibt zu) |gab zu, zugegeben|
9. **to interrupt** unterbrechen |unterbrach, unterbrochen|
10. **to translate** übersetzen

Example Sentences
1. **His was (being) judged by the jury.** Er wurde von der Jury verurteilt.
2. **The bathroom is (being) occupied.** Das Badezimmer ist besetzt.
3. **The paper is (being) folded.** Das Papier wird gefaltet.
4. **The city was (being) conquered.** Die Stadt wurde erobert.
5. **She is (being) convinced.** Sie wird überzeugt.
6. **The lip was (being) bitten.** Die Lippe wurde gebissen.
7. **We are (being) protected.** Wir werden beschützt.
8. **The truth was (being) admitted.** Die Wahrheit wurde zugegeben.
9. **The meeting was (being) interrupted.** Die Sitzung wurde unterbrochen.
10. **The book is (being) translated.** Das Buch wird übersetzt.

Day 78: Passive Voice Part 2

Today's lesson covers the Statal or False Passive. This is used to show the resultant state of a past action. There are two constructions in both English and German, one that focuses on the end result, and one that focuses on the change itself. To focus on the end result, replace the auxiliary *werden* with *sein.* Since this grammar shows a result, it can not take the translation *being*, because the action is already completed. Study the following examples:

The doughnut is eaten.	Der Donut ist gegessen.
The doughnut was eaten.	Der Doughnut war gegessen.
The coffee is made.	Der Kaffee ist gemacht.
The coffee was made.	Der Kaffee war gemacht.

The far more common grammar is to focus on the change itself. English uses the construction (to have) + *been* + (past participle). German uses (sein) + (past participle) + *worden. Worden* is the participle of *werden* without the *ge-* prefix. Study the following examples:

The doughnut has been eaten.	Der Donut ist gegessen worden.
The doughnut had been eaten.	Der Donut war gegessen worden.
The coffee has been made.	Der Kaffee ist gemacht worden.
The coffee had been made.	Der Kaffee war gemacht worden.

Though *worden* is the translation of *been*, it is only used in passive sentences that show a change in state. Be careful not to use it in translations of English continuous tense sentences. Remember that German sentences have multiple tense translations in English. Study the following example:

I have been going.	(correct) Ich bin gegangen. (incorrect) Ich bin worden gehen.

Be careful with translations of modal verbs as well. Modal verbs using *have been* in English have a completely different meaning. For example, the phrase *could have been* has nothing to do with ability, but rather speculation, and will use Konjunktiv II.

The doughnut could have been eaten.	(correct) Der Donut hätte gegessen werden können. (incorrect) Der Donut konnte gegessen worden sein.

Day 78 Grammar Card

1. **Statal passive (end result focus)**
(sein) + (past participle)
2. **Statal passive (change focus)**
(sein) + (past participle) + worden

Day 78 Vocabulary

1. **to resolve / settle** klären
**Kläre*n* literally means *to clear.* English can use this translation as well: *I cleared my debt. The issue was cleared.* Another meaning is, *to check with someone to see if something is okay*, as in: *I cleared it with the boss.*
2. **to improve** verbessern
3. **to describe** beschreiben |beschrieb, beschrieben|
4. **to prevent / hinder** verhindern
5. **to take over** übernehmen (übernimmt) |übernahm, übernommen|
**Übernehmen* means *to take over*, but can also be translated as *to adopt*, as in *a policy* or *a plan.*
6. **to emphasize / point out** betonen
7. **to expect** erwarten
8. **to combine / unite** vereinen
9. **to represent** vertreten (vertritt) |vertrat, vertreten|
10. **to support / assist** unterstützen

Example Sentences

1. **The problem has been settled.** Das Problem ist geklärt worden.
2. **It has been improved every day.** Es ist jeden Tag verbessert worden.
3. **It had been described to her.** Es war ihr beschrieben worden.
4. **The attack has been prevented.** Der Angriff ist verhindert worden.
5. **The country had been taken over.** Das Land war übernommen worden.
6. **The point has been emphasized.** Der Punkt ist betont worden.
7. **The result had been expected.** Das Ergebnis war erwartet worden.
8. **The people have been united.** Die Menschen sind vereint worden.
9. **The countries have been represented.** Die Länder sind vertreten worden.
10. **The idea had been supported.** Die Idee war unterstützt worden.

Day 79: Passive Voice Part 3

The future passive in English uses the construction *will be* + (past participle). German uses (werden) + (past particle) + *werden*. Study the following examples:

| The doughnut will be eaten. | Der Donut wird gegessen werden. |
| The coffee will be made. | Der Kaffee wird gemacht werden. |

Modal verbs will be sent to the end of the sentence. Study the following examples:

| The doughnut will be able to be eaten. | Der Donut wird gegessen werden können. |
| The coffee will have to be made. | Der Kaffee wird gemacht werden müssen. |

The future past passive in English uses the construction *will have been* + (past participle). German uses (werden) + (past particle) + *worden sein*. Study the following examples:

| The doughnut will have been eaten. | Der Donut wird gegessen worden sein. |
| The coffee will have been made. | Der Kaffee wird gemacht worden sein. |

Modal verbs will be sent to the end of the sentence, but again, using *have been* will change the meaning of most modal verbs, so this grammar is extremely rare and can only be used in very specific cases.

| The doughnut will be able to have been eaten. | Der Donut wird gegessen worden sein können. |
| The coffee will have to have been made. | Der Kaffee wird gemacht worden sein müssen. |

If you're having trouble remember passive word order, there is a cool trick. Put a number next to each verb. The auxiliary verb is in the same position, but all the other verbs are in the opposite order at the end of the sentence. If you want to think like a German, all you have to do is think backwards! Study the following example:

| 1) will 2) have 3) been 4) eaten | 1) wird 4) gegessen 3) worden 2) sein |
| 1) will 2) be able to 3) have 4) been 5) eaten | 1) wird 5) gegessen 4) worden 3) sein 2) können |

Day 79 Grammar Cards:
1. **Future passive**
(werden) + (past participle) + werden
2. **Future passive (modal)**
(werden) + (past participle) + werden + (modal)
3. **Future past passive**
(werden) + (past participle) + worden sein
4. **Future past passive (modal)**
(werden) + (past participle) + worden sein (modal)

Day 79 Vocabulary
1. **to report *on*** berichten *von*
2. **to renew / remake / modernize** erneuern
3. **to dig** graben (gräbt) |grub, gegraben|
4. **to exclude** aus'nehmen (nimmt aus) |nahm aus, ausgenommen|
5. **to give (a present)** schenken
6. **to perform / enact** auf'führen
7. **to reward** belohnen
8. **to activate** ein'schalten
9. **to confirm** bestätigen
10. **to produce** her'stellen

Example Sentences
1. **The news will be reported.** Die Nachrichten werden berichtet werden.
2. **The license will be renewed.** Der Führerschein wird erneuert werden.
3. **The hole will have been dug.** Das Loch wird gegraben worden sein.
4. **It can be excluded.** Es kann ausgenommen werden.
5. **A present ought to be given.** Ein Geschenk soll geschenkt werden.
6. **The play will be performed.** Das Theaterstück wird aufgeführt werden.
7. **Patience will be rewarded.** Geduld wird belohnt.
8. **The program will have been activated.** Das Programm wird eingeschaltet worden sein.
9. **The report will have to be confirmed.** Der Report wird bestätigt werden müssen.
10. **The products will be produced.** Die Ware wird hergestellt werden.

You may be asking, why did we learn Konjunktiv II before Konjunktiv I? I asked that very same question, and no one knows! Whoever decided to call this grammar Konjunktiv I made a mistake, because Konjunktiv II is used far more often.

Konjunktiv I is used for reported speech, to let the listener know that these words are not your own, you are only reporting them. You see it a lot in the news. English doesn't differentiate grammar when quoting someone else, but German does. In everyday conversations, it isn't necessary to explicitly say that you are reporting, and most speakers won't use this grammar even when quoting someone.

Irregular verbs <u>do not</u> have a vowel change when conjugated into Konjunktiv I. Simply drop the *-en* and add the following endings:

Konjunktiv I			
ich	-e	wir	-en
du	-est	ihr	-et
er	-e	sie	-en
sie	-e	Sie	-en
es	-e		

Sein has an irregular Konjunktiv I conjugation:

(sein) Konjunktiv I			
ich	sei	wir	seien
du	seist	ihr	seiet
er	sei	sie	seien
sie	sei	Sie	seien
es	sei		

1. **Reported speech**

No vowel change. Drop -*en* add:

Konjunktiv I			
ich	-e	wir	-en
du	-est	ihr	-et
er	-e	sie	-en
sie	-e	Sie	-en
es	-e		

2.

(sein) Konjunktiv I			
ich	sei	wir	seien
du	seist	ihr	seiet
er	sei	sie	seien
sie	sei	Sie	seien
es	sei		

Day 80 Vocabulary

1. **still / yet** noch
2. **really / actually** wirklich
3. **maybe** vielleicht
4. **just / straight / directly / exactly** gerade

Gerade is used with time as in *just now*. It is also used with directions to say *straight*.

5. **of course / naturally** natürlich
6. **idea / hunch / premonition** die Ahnung (-en)
7. **rather / quite / somewhat** ziemlich
8. **completely / totally** völlig
9. **by chance / randomly** zufällig
10. **by the way / incidentally** übrigens

Example Sentences

1. **He said he still hasn't come.** Er sagte, er sei noch nicht gekommen.
2. **She asked if he actually went to the party.** Sie fragte, ob er wirklich zur Party gegangen sei.
3. **He said that she might come.** Er sagte, dass sie vielleicht komme.
4. **They said they have just arrived.** Sie sagten, dass sie gerade angekommen seien.
5. **She said, of course, they all are eating sausage.** Sie sagte, dass ihr natürlich Würstchen esset.
6. **She said she has no idea.** Sie sagte sie habe keine Ahnung.
7. **He thinks it tastes rather good.** Er meinte es schmecke ziemlich gut.
8. **They said it was completely different.** Sie sagten es sei völlig anders gewesen.
9. **He said it happens randomly.** Er sagte es passiere zufällig.
10. **By the way, she asked, can you come?** Übrigens hat sie gefragt, ob du kommen könnest?

Day 81: Prefixes

Like in English, German prefixes have a general meaning. For example, the prefix *pre-* means *before*. It isn't necessary to memorize these, but if you can recall the general meaning of prefixes, it will help you distinguish similar vocabulary words. For example, you have previously studied the word *packen* (to pack). If you know *ein-* means *in*, and *aus-* means *out*, you can derive the meaning of the words *einpacken* (to pack up) and *auspacken* (to unpack) without looking them up. Of course, some of the meanings are far more abstract, like *aufhören* (to stop), but even with words like this you can use the prefix meanings to create a mnemonic: *Stop* what you are doing and *listen up*!

Prefix Meanings			
ab-	away from	**mit-**	with
an-	at / on / to / toward	**nach-**	after / follow / copy
auf-	on / open / up / finish	**nieder-**	down / lower
aus-	out / extend / off	**über-**	over / too much / failure
be-	effecting / grasping	**um-**	around / down / over
bei-	along / with	**ver-**	make worse / opposite / bad
durch-	through	**voll-**	full / complete
ein-	in / into	**vor-**	ahead / before / pre-
emp-	upward / receive	**weg-**	away
ent-	away from / separate / oppose	**wider-**	against / oppose
er-	completed / fatal	**wieder-**	again
fort-	away / continue	**zer-**	destroy / shatter / collapse
her-	hither / from / toward	**zu-**	close / shut
hin-	down / to / away from	**zurück-**	back / re-
hinter-	behind	**zusammen-**	together
miss-	failure		

Day 81 Vocabulary
1. **to expire / run out** ab'laufen (läuft ab) |lief ab, abgelaufen|
2. **to teach / provide** bei'bringen |brachte bei, beigebracht|
3. **to sense / feel** empfinden |empfand, empfunden|
4. **to go with / accompany** mit'gehen |ging mit, mitgegangen|
5. **to copy / clone / reproduce** nach'bilden
6. **to connect / combine** verbinden |verband, verbunden|
7. **to leave / go away** weg'gehen |ging weg, weggegangen|
8. **to break apart / disassemble** zerlegen
9. **to return / come back** zurück'kommen |kam zurück. zurückgekommen|
10. **to be related / associated** zusammen'hängen |hing zusammen, zusammengehangen|

Example Sentences
1. **The milk has expired.** Die Milch ist abgelaufen.
2. **Can you teach me German?** Kannst du mir Deutsch beibringen?
3. **He felt a deep sadness.** Er empfand eine tiefe Traue.
4. **Will you go with us?** Wirst du mit uns mitgehen?
5. **They copied the Titanic one for one.** Sie haben die Titanic eins zu eins nachgebildet.
6. **The computer is not connected to the network.** Der Computer is nicht mit dem Netzwerk verbunden.
7. **Go away!** Geh weg!
8. **I took the toy apart.** Ich habe das Spielzeug zerlegt.
9. **When are you all coming back?** Wann kommt ihr zurück?
10. **These two are related.** Diese Zwei hängen zusammen.

Day 82: Suffixes

German suffixes don't have such abstract core meanings as the prefixes, and can usually translate one to one into English. It's actually a good idea to memorize these, because they will show up a lot. There is also one idiomatic expression using the suffix -los: *Was ist los?* (What's the matter?).

Suffix Meanings	
-artig	-like
-bar	-able
-chen / -lein	small / young
-haft	Emphasizes root word.
-heim	home
-heit / -keit	-ness
-ig	-y / in a certain way
-isch	-ish
-ismus	-ism
-lich	-ly
-los	-less, without
-reich / -voll	plenty
-sam	-some
-schaft	-ship
-ung	Changes verbs into nouns.
-wert / -würdig	worth doing

Day 82 Grammar Card
1. **What's the matter? / What's wrong?**
Was ist los?

Day 82 Vocabulary
1. **brilliant / excellent** großartig
2. **visible / recognizable** erkennbar
3. **credible / believable** glaubwürdig
4. **loneliness** die Einsamkeit
5. **capitalism** der Kapitalismus
6. **helpless** hilflos
7. **successful** erfolgreich
8. **thrifty / cheap** sparsam
9. **friendship** die Freundschaft (-en)
10. **landmark/sight seeing place** die Sehenswürdigkeit (-en)

Example Sentences
1. **That's brilliant!** Das ist großartig!
2. **This is unrecognizable.** Das ist unerkennbar.
3. **This report is not credible.** Dieser Bericht ist nicht glaubwürdig.
4. **It's hard to cope with loneliness.** Es ist schwer, mit der Einsamkeit zurechtzukommen.
5. **Capitalism is an economic system.** Kapitalismus ist eine Wirtschaftsform.
6. **I always feel helpless.** Ich fühle mich immer hilflos.
7. **I want to be successful.** Ich will erfolgreich sein.
8. **I am thrifty because I need to save.** Ich bin sparsam, weil ich sparen muss.
9. **I value friendship.** Freundschaft ist mir sehr wichtig.
10. **Are there many sights to see?** Gibt es viele Sehenswürdigkeiten zu sehen?

Day 83: Weak Nouns

There is a special class of masculine nouns called Weak Nouns. They are weak because -n or -en is added when the noun is not in the nominative case. It's not really necessary to memorize these words, but in your studies, you may come across a noun that has an -n attached, that isn't plural, and wonder why that is. It's because that noun is weak. Some of the more common weak nouns are *der Herr, der Mensch, der Name*. Study the following examples:

I gave the gentleman a tip.	Ich gab dem Herren einen Hinweis.
Human greed has no end.	Die Gier des Menschen ist endlos.
I don't know her name.	Ich kenne ihren Namen nicht.

Day 83 Vocabulary
All of today's vocabulary words are weak nouns.
1. **bear** der Bär (-en)
2. **messenger** der Bote (-n)
3. **letter (alphabet)** der Buchstabe (-n)
4. **adult** der Erwachsene (-n)
5. **belief** der Glaube (-n)
6. **customer** der Kunde (-n)
7. **soldier** der Soldat (-en)
8. **lion** der Löwe (-n)
9. **hero** der Held (-en)
10. **relative (family)** der Verwandte (-n)

Example Sentences
1. **Do you see the bear?** Siehst du den Bären?
2. **Don't shoot the messenger.** Erschieß den Boten nicht.
3. **I can't read the letters.** Ich kann den Buchstaben nicht lesen.
4. **Please work with an adult.** Arbeiten Sie bitte mit einem Erwachsenen.
5. **I don't understand this belief.** Ich verstehe diesen Glauben nicht.
6. **I serve the same customer every day.** Ich bediene jeden Tag den gleichen Kunden.
7. **He knows the soldier.** Er kennt den Soldaten.
8. **Don't play with the lion's tail.** Spiel nicht mit dem Schwanz des Löwen.
9. **She needs a hero.** Sie braucht einen Helden.
10. **I have no relatives.** Ich habe keine Verwandten.

Day 84: False Cognates Part 1

There are many German and English cognates, so learning vocabulary can be quite easy. However, there are also many false cognates. These are words that seem to be the same in both languages, but are actually different. The moral of today's lesson is that you should always look up a word that you encounter for the first time, because even though it might look similar to an English word, or you think you might know the meaning, it could be completely different.

Day 84 Vocabulary
1. **to graduate / complete a class** absolvieren
2. **current / up to date** aktuell
3. **poison** das Gift (-e)
4. **high school** das Gymnasium (die Gymnasien)
5. **college** die Hochschule (-n)
6. **cell phone** das Handy (-s)
7. **bank deposit / bail money** die Kaution (-en)
8. **consistently** konsequent
9. **strange / quaint** kurios
10. **room and board** Kost und Logis
*The word order is switched. Germans say *board and room*.

Example Sentences
1. **I have completed the course.** Ich habe den Kurs absolviert.
2. **Is this report up to date?** Ist dieser Bericht aktuell?
3. **Romeo drank the poison.** Romeo trank das Gift.
4. **High school is tough.** Das Gymnasium ist hart.
5. **Did you go to college?** Bist du auf die Hochschule gegangen?
6. **I don't have a cell phone.** Ich habe kein Handy.
7. **The bail is very expensive.** Die Kaution ist sehr hoch.
8. **The results are consistent with logic.** Die Ergebnisse sind logisch konsequent.
9. **What a strange child.** Was ein kurioses Kind.
10. **How much is room and board?** Wie viel für Kost und Logis?

Day 85: False Cognates Part 2

<u>Day 85 Vocabulary</u>
1. **bar / restaurant / business** das Lokal (-e)
2. **manure / dung** der Mist
3. **distress** die Not (ö,-e)
Not is often used in compound words to indicate difficulty or distress. For example: *die Atemnot* (difficulty breathing).
4. **vulgar / uncouth** ordinär
5. **motto / slogan** die Parole (-n)
6. **bed and breakfast hotel** die Pension (-en)
7. **hot chilies / peppers** die Peperoni
8. **pimple** der Pickel
9. **commission / fee** die Provision (-en)
10. **trial / law suit** der Prozess (-e)

<u>Example Sentences</u>
1. **That's a good place.** Das is ein gutes Lokal.
2. **Manure smells really bad.** Der Mist riecht sehr schlecht.
3. **In case of emergency, call the police.** Im Notfall, rufen Sie die Polizei.
4. **How vulgar!** Wie ordinär!
5. **They fought the communists with the slogan: Power to the people!** Sie bekämpften den Kommunismus unter der Parole: Alle Macht dem Volke!
6. **I slept at a bed and breakfast.** Ich schlief in einer Pension.
7. **I like pizza with peppers.** Ich mag Pizza mit Peperoni.
8. **I hate pimples!** Ich hasse Pickel!
9. **I got a big commission.** Ich habe eine hohe Provision bekommen.
10. **The trial takes place tomorrow.** Der Prozess findet morgen statt.

Day 86: False Cognates Part 3

<u>Day 86 Vocabulary</u>
1. **fumes / smoke** der Qualm
2. **rate / quota** die Quote (-n)
3. **advice** der Rat
4. **novel** der Roman (-e)
5. **sparkling wine** der Sekt (-e)
6. **sensitive** sensibel
7. **reliable / legitimate** seriös
8. **tuxedo** der Smoking (-s)
9. **forklift** der Stapler
10. **likable / personable** sympathisch

<u>Example Sentences</u>
1. **Smoke came out of the ground.** Qualm kam aus der Erde.
2. **Can you tell me the rate?** Kannst du mir die Quote sagen?
3. **I don't need your advice.** Ich brauche deinen Rat nicht.
4. **Did you read the novel?** Hast du den Roman gelesen?
5. **I like to drink sparkling wine.** Ich trinke gern Sekt.
6. **I am a sensitive person.** Ich bin ein sensibler Mensch.
7. **This report is not legitimate.** Dieser Bericht ist nicht seriös.
8. **He is wearing a tuxedo.** Er trägt einen Smoking.
9. **The forklift is quite large.** Der Stapler ist ziemlich groß.
10. **He is likable.** Er ist sympatisch.

Day 87: Numbers Part 1

The numbers in German aren't hard to remember, some of them are cognates. All numbers in German are feminine, but certain regions have some masculine numbers. Number gender isn't so important as you will likely never say a number with an article, but if you must, use feminine as your default. Study the following list:

0	null	10	zehn
1	eins	11	elf
2	zwei	12	zwölf
3	drei	13	dreizehn
4	vier	14	vierzehn
5	fünf	15	fünfzehn
6	sechs	16	sechzehn
7	sieben	17	siebzehn
8	acht	18	achtzehn
9	neun	19	neunzehn

The deca-numbers add -*zig* or -*ßig,* and are said backwards, with an added *and,* all as one word, no spaces. Study the following examples:

20	zwanzig
30	dreißig
40	vierzig
50	fünfzig
60	sechzig
70	siebzig
80	achtzig
90	neunzig
25	fünfundzwanzig
32	zweiunddreißig
87	siebenundachtzig

Hundreds and thousands translate one to one into English, but again have no spaces in the spellings. English sometimes adds *a* or *one* to these numbers, but that isn't necessary in German:

100	hundert
1000	tausend
500	fünfhundert
9000	neuntausend

Numbers over a million are capitalized, and have two versions for each comma added. Unless you are talking about the national debt of some countries, you may never use numbers this big.

million	Million	1,000,000
billion	Milliarde	1,000,000,000
trillion	Billion	1,000,000,000,000
quadrillion	Billiarde	1,000,000,000,000,000

Commas and decimal points take the opposite position in German. Study the following examples:

3.14159	3,14159
1,234,567.89	1.234.567,89

1. **Sunday** der Sonntag (-e)
2. **Monday** der Montag (-e)
3. **Tuesday** der Dienstag (-e)
4. **Wednesday** der Mittwoch (-e)
5. **Thursday** der Donnerstag (-e)
6. **Friday** der Freitag (-e)
7. **Saturday** der Samstag (-e)
8. **day** der Tag (-e)
9. **every day** jeden Tag
10. **week** die Woche (n)

Example Sentences

1. **I go to church on Sundays.** Ich gehe sonntags in die Kirche.
*To say *on ~days*, simply add an *-s* to the day and change the capital letter to a lower case letter.
2. **I hate Mondays.** Ich hasse Montage.
*Notice this sentence didn't say *on Mondays*.
3. **On Tuesdays we eat hamburgers.** Dienstags essen wir Hamburger.
4. **What are you doing on Wednesday?** Was machst du am Mittwoch?
5. **Thursday is almost here.** Es ist fast schon Donnerstag.
6. **Fridays are really fun.** Freitage machen viel Spaß.
7. **They are coming on Saturday.** Sie kommen am Samstag.
8. **Today is the day.** Heute ist der Tag.
9. **I drink milk every day.** Ich trinke jeden Tag Milch.
10. **What are you all doing this week?** Was macht ihr diese Woche?

Day 88: Numbers Part 2

Math is relatively simple in German. Like English, there are many ways to say equations. German can use *gleich* (equals), *ist* (is), or *macht* (makes).

Addition uses the word *plus* (plus) or *und* (and). Study the following examples:

One and one is two.	Eins und eins ist zwei.
Two plus two equals four.	Zwei plus zwei gleich vier.

Subtraction uses *minus* (minus) or *weniger* (less). Study the following examples:

Six minus three is three.	Sechs minus drei ist drei.
Ten less than ten makes zero.	Zehn weniger zehn macht null.

Multiplication uses *mal* (times). Study the following examples:

Ten times ten is a hundred.	Zehn mal zehn ist hundert.
Three times three equals nine.	Drei mal drei gleich neun.

Division uses *durch* (through). Study the following examples:

Eight divided by two makes four.	Acht durch zwei macht vier.
Nine divided by three is three.	Neun durch drei ist drei.

1. **to calculate / estimate** rechnen
2. **number** die Zahl (-en)
3. **to pay** bezahlen
4. **to count** zählen

Zählen has the nuance of validity, like in English. For example: *Das zählt nicht.* (That doesn't count.)

5. **bill / calculation** die Rechnung (-en)
6. **times** mal

Mal is also used to indicate how many times: *einmal* (once), *zweimal* (twice). It is also used in the phrase *noch einmal* (one more time).

7. **to separate / split / share** teilen
8. **to separate / chop / break up** trennen

*The reflexive *sich trennen* is used to separate yourself from something, like a relationship. For example: *Ich trenne mich von dir.* (I am breaking up with you.)

9. **to compare** *to* vergleichen *mit* |verglich, verglichen|
10. **remaining / left over** übrig

Example Sentences
1. **Can you calculate that?** Kannst du das rechnen?
2. **What is your favorite number?** Was ist Ihre Lieblingszahl?
3. **We have to pay.** Wir müssen bezahlen.
4. **I count three members.** Ich zähle drei Mitglieder.
5. **May I see the bill?** Darf ich die Rechnung sehen?
6. **Three times three is nine.** Drei mal drei ist neun.
7. **Let's split the bill.** Lass uns die Rechnung teilen.
8. **I can't separate it.** Ich kann es nicht trennen.
9. **They are comparing their answers.** Sie vergleichen ihre Antworten.
10. **How much is left?** Wie viel ist übrig?

Day 89: Dates

There are two ways to ask for the date in German. The latter example is more natural:

What is the date?	Was ist das Datum?	
What is the date?	Welches Datum haben wir heute?	Lit. What date do we have today?

English adds -*th* to numbers to make them dates or ranks. German adds -*te*, or -*ste* (deca-numbers). There are two exceptions, *erste* (first), and *dritte* (third). Though the numbers themselves are feminine, dates are masculine.

first	erste
second	zweite
third	dritte
fourth	vierte
fifth	fünfte
sixth	sechste
seventh	siebte
eighth	achte
ninth	neunte
tenth	zehnte
twentieth	zwanzigste
thirtieth	dreißigste

The day will always come first when saying dates. When this is done in English, *of* is added, but German doesn't add a preposition. To say *on the*, German uses *an*, which takes the dative case, and since dates are masculine, will become *am* (an + dem). Study the following examples:

On the first.	Am ersten.
The first of January.	Der erste Januar.
On the fourth of July.	Am vierten Juli.
On the twenty-fifth of December.	Am fünfundzwanzigsten Dezember.

Like English, years by themselves take the preposition *in* in the dative case, which becomes *im* (in + dem) and will also add *Jahre* (year). Like English, if you are saying a complete date with the day, month, and year, you don't need a preposition. Study the following examples:

In two thousand ten.	Im Jahre zweitausendzehn.
On the twenty-fifth of December, two thousand ten.	Am fünfundzwanzigsten Dezember, zweitausendzehn.
Today is May seventh, two thousand three.	Heute ist der siebte Mai zweitausenddrei.

Day 89 Grammar Cards
1. **Dates or ranks (-th)**
Masculine. Add *-te* / *-ste* (deca-numbers)
2. **first / third**
erste / dritte
3. **on the (date)**
am (date)
4. **in (year)**
im Jahre (year)

Day 89 Vocabulary
1. **to celebrate** feiern
2. **holiday** der Feiertag (-e)
3. **glad** froh
*Also used in the phrases: *Frohes neues Jahr* (Happy New Year) and *Frohe Weihnachten* (Merry Christmas).
4. **date** das Datum (die Daten)
5. **to relax** sich entspannen
6. **to rest** sich ausruhen
7. **to calm down** sich beruhigen
8. **vacation** der Urlaub (-e)
*English uses the preposition *on* with vacation, German uses *in*. To say *take a vacation*, use the verb *fahren* or *gehen*.
9. **autumn** der Herbst (-e)
10. **spring** der Frühling (e)

Example Sentences
1. **Do you celebrate Christmas?** Feierst du Weihnachten?
2. **What is your favorite holiday?** Was ist dein Lieblingsfeiertag?
3. **He is always glad.** Er ist immer froh.
4. **What is the date today?** Welches Datum haben wir heute?
5. **I have to relax more.** Ich muss mich mehr entspannen.
6. **Sometimes I rest in the living room.** Manchmal ruhe ich mich im Wohnzimmer aus.
7. **She needs to calm down.** Sie muss sich beruhigen.
8. **He is on vacation.** Er ist im Urlaub.
9. **I take a vacation in autumn.** Im Herbst fahre ich in den Urlaub.
10. **Spring is so beautiful.** Der Frühling ist so schön.

Day 90: Time

Time flies when you are having fun! In German culture, being on time is very important. The most important time vocabulary word is *die Uhr* (time / clock / watch / o'clock). Like dates, there are two ways to ask for the time. Study the following examples:

What time is it?	Wie spät ist es?	Lit. How late is it?
What time is it?	Wie viel Uhr ist es?	Lit. How much time is it?

Uhr is always said after the hour. Study the following examples:

It is three forty.	Es ist drei Uhr vierzig.
It is seven o'clock.	Es ist sieben Uhr.

Most time expressions can be directly translated. The exception is *thirty*. German also uses the next hour plus the word *halb* (half). Most prepositions can be directly translated as well, for example: *nach* (after) *von* (from) and *bis* (until). Study the following examples:

It is nine thirty.	Es ist halb zehn. Es ist neun Uhr dreißig.
It is a quarter after two.	Es ist Viertel nach zwei.
It is a quarter before eight.	Es ist Viertel vor acht.
I'll wait until six o'clock.	Ich warte bis sechs Uhr.

Some prepositions with time don't directly translate. Study the following list and examples:

Time Prepositions	
since / for	seit
at	um
around	gegen
ago	vor

I have been living in Germany for two years.	Ich wohne seit zwei Jahren in Deutschland.
I have been living in Germany since 1995.	Ich wohne seit 1995 in Deutschland.
It starts at seven.	Es fängt um sieben Uhr an.
We are meeting around eight.	Wir treffen uns gegen acht Uhr.
I went to Germany four years ago.	Ich bin vor vier Jahren nach Deutschland gegangen.

1. **What time is it?**
Wie spät ist es?
Wie viel Uhr ist es?
2. **(hour) (minute)**
(hour) Uhr (minute)
3. **(hour) thirty**
halb (hour + 1)
4. **since / for, at, around, ago**
seit, um, gegen, vor

Day 90 Vocabulary
1. **clock / watch / time** die Uhr
2. **today** heute
3. **yesterday** gestern
4. **tomorrow / morning** morgen
5. **time** die Zeit (-en)
6. **year** das Jahr (-e)
7. **month** der Monat (-e)
8. **now** jetzt
9. **late** spät
10. **early** früh

Example Sentences
1. **I don't have a watch.** Ich habe keine Uhr.
2. **Today is Saturday.** Heute ist Samstag.
3. **Yesterday was Friday.** Gestern war Freitag.
4. **Tomorrow is Sunday.** Morgen ist Sonntag.
5. **Time passes so quickly.** Die Zeit vergeht so schnell.
6. **This year I'm traveling to Germany.** Dieses Jahr reise ich nach Deutschland.
7. **Next month she is moving.** Nächsten Monat zieht sie um.
8. **I am coming now.** Ich komme jetzt.
9. **We are starting late today.** Wir fangen heute spät an.
10. **Class ends early today.** Der Unterricht endet heute früh.

Congratulations!

You've finished the book, great job! The question is, now what? You are now a high beginner level speaker of German. The lessons in the book are a summary of everything you would learn in two years of a college level German class. To progress to intermediate and advanced, you're going to have to work on a few things.

The difference between an advanced speaker and everyone else is your level of vocabulary and your speaking speed. You may find that you now know all the basic rules of grammar, but it takes a bit of time to form sentences, to answer questions, to understand what you hear and read. To increase your speed, you're going to need to review. If you spend the next 90 days reviewing each lesson one more time, reviewing the vocabulary and grammar, I guarantee you will be able to recall the information much faster. After another 90 days of review, I think you could call yourself an intermediate level speaker.

To become an advanced speaker, you're going to have to get a little more serious. Assuming your grammar skills are honed, the next hurdle is vocabulary. A fluent speaker should be able to recall around 5000 words. If you follow the 10 word a day method, this could take up to 500 days, or more realistically, about two years. One question you might have is where to find new vocabulary. The answer is reading. Get a book, a newspaper, anything written. Read a paragraph once through without looking up any of the words. Read it <u>out loud</u>. Go back and find ten words that you didn't know, make a note card with these words. Continue doing this each day.

Unfortunately, no matter how much you study, no matter how much you practice, you will never be a fluent speaker unless you go to Germany, unless you speak with natives. In this book I have tried to include the most important rules of grammar, but there are still more. There are little nuances and rules that you still need to learn, things you won't learn unless you surround yourself with German speakers. The German language, like every language, is constantly changing. Different regions have different vocabulary and accents and dialects. These things can not be learned in a book, they can only be learned by experience. So get out there, go to a German speaking country, make German speaking friends! I wish you the best of luck in all your future studies and endeavors.

Study hard! Study every day!
-KM